Reflective Practice in TESOL Service-Learning

Reflective Practice in Language Education
Series Editor: Thomas S. C. Farrell, Brock University

This series covers different issues related to reflective practice in language education and includes an introductory book which introduces these areas. The other books in the series clarify the different approaches that have been taken within reflective practice and outline current themes that have emerged in the research on various topics and methods of reflection that have occurred.

Published:

Reflective Practice in ELT
Thomas S. C. Farrell

Cooperative Learning through a Reflective Lens
George M. Jacobs, Anita Lie and Siti Mina Tamah

Micro-Reflection on Classroom Communication: A FAB Framework
Hansun Zhang Waring and Sarah Chepkirui Creider

Reflecting on Leadership in Language Education
Edited by Andy Curtis

Using Video to Support Teacher Reflection and Development in ELT
Laura Baecher, Steve Mann and Cecilia Nobre

Forthcoming:

English Language Teacher Beliefs
Farahnaz Faez and Michael Karas

Exploring the Principles of Reflective Practice in ELT: Research and Perspectives from Turkey
Edited by Bahar Gün and Evrim Üstünlüoğlu

Language Teacher Identity and Reflective Practice
Zia Tajeddin

Surviving the Induction Years of Language Teaching: The Importance of Reflective Practice
Thomas S. C. Farrell

Teachers Reflecting on Boredom in the Language Classroom
Mirosław Pawlak, Mariusz Kruk and Joanna Zawodniak

The Reflective Cycle of the Teaching Practicum
Fiona Farr and Angela Farrell

Reflective Practice in TESOL Service-Learning

Cynthia J. Macknish

UNIVERSITY OF TORONTO PRESS

Toronto Buffalo London

Reprinted 2025 by University of Toronto Press
Toronto Buffalo London
utppublishing.com
Printed in the USA

First published 2023 by Equinox Publishing Ltd.
© Cynthia J. Macknish 2023

British Library Cataloguing-in-Publication Data
A catalogue record for this book is available from the British Library.

ISBN-13   978 1 80050 306 9   (hardback)
          978 1 80050 307 6   (paperback)
          978 1 80050 308 3   (ePDF)
          978 1 80050 351 9   (ePub)

Library of Congress Cataloging-in-Publication Data

Names: Macknish, Cynthia, author.
Title: Reflective practice in TESOL service-learning / Cynthia J. Macknish.

Description: Sheffield, South Yorkshire ; Bristol, CT : Equinox Publishing
  Ltd., 2023. | Series: Reflective practice in language education |
  Includes bibliographical references. | Summary: "This book provides both
  theory and practical tools for TESOL educators (and others) to use as
  they guide pre-service teachers of English to reflect in meaningful ways
  in a service-learning context. Interpretations of service-learning are
  presented along with the crucial role that reflective practice plays in
  it. Challenges in defining and implementing reflective practice in TESOL
  service-learning contexts are explored and practical tools and
  strategies to help address them are shared"-- Provided by publisher.
Identifiers: LCCN 2022046917 (print) | LCCN 2022046918 (ebook) | ISBN
  9781800503069 (hardback) | ISBN 9781800503076 (paperback) | ISBN
  9781800503083 (pdf) | ISBN 9781800503519 (epub)
Subjects: LCSH: English language--Study and teaching--Foreign speakers. |
  Reflective teaching. | English teachers--Training of.
Classification: LCC PE1128.A2 M236 2023 (print) | LCC PE1128.A2 (ebook) |
  DDC 428.0071--dc23/eng/20230216
LC record available at https://lccn.loc.gov/2022046917
LC ebook record available at https://lccn.loc.gov/2022046918

Cover image courtesy of Davide Boscolo / Unsplash
Design: Mark Lee / hisandhers.design
Typeset by Sparks Publishing Services Ltd – www.sparkspublishing.com

Contents

Acknowledgments

I am deeply grateful to the preservice teachers in my TESOL courses for sharing their thinking about their service-learning experience, for teaching me more about effective reflection, and for giving me permission to use excerpts from their reflections to help others.

Series Editor's Preface

Service-learning is defined by the National Service-Learning Clearinghouse as "a teaching and learning strategy that integrates meaningful community service with instruction and reflection to enrich the learning experience, teach civic responsibility, and strengthen communities" (cited in Ryan, 2012, p. 4). An essential part of service-learning pedagogy is reflective practice. Thus the latest book in the series *Reflective Practice in Language Education* by Cynthia J. Macknish, *Reflective Practice in TESOL Service-Learning* actually combines many goals of both reflective practice and service-learning. These common goals include constructing meaning, improving teaching and learning, developing self-awareness and a disposition of inquiry, changing understandings, and motivating change.

This book offers TESOL educators and others who implement service-learning in their programs some insight into what reflective practice in TESOL service-learning might look like. It points to the many benefits of well-designed service-learning experiences for preservice and experienced ESOL teachers that include increased awareness of academic and pedagogical issues, development of ELT skills and strategies. understanding and reinforcement of theory–practice connections, improved skills in reflection and critical thinking, enhanced self-awareness and sense of personal and professional identity, greater cultural and linguistic awareness and empathy, increased awareness of diversity and social justice issues, development of experience and confidence working with culturally and linguistically diverse learners, and many more. In addition, many benefits are extended for community partners and multilingual learners that really make a service-learning approach with reflective practice unique in the field of teaching English to speakers of other languages. These include additional linguistic support, additional social support, improved academic success, increased confidence, stronger motivation and positive attitude toward language learning, and increased sense of community often lacking in other more traditional approaches to teacher learning and development.

The book also offers practical tools and strategies that are presented to help foster a strong form of reflective practice with preservice or inservice teachers in TESOL service-learning programs.

The book consists of seven user-friendly written chapters. Chapter 1, What is Service-Learning? explains many of the theoretical foundations of service-learning as well as its value and importance in TESOL contexts. Chapter 2, Characterizing Reflective Practice in TESOL Service-Learning, outlines and discusses how reflective practice, and especially critical reflection, is characterized in service-learning in terms of the purpose and principles involved. Chapter 3, Analyzing and Assessing Reflections in TESOL Service-Learning, outlines the various goals, outcomes, and objectives in TESOL service-learning, followed by a presentation of several models of reflection analysis. Chapter 4, Facilitating Reflective Practice in TESOL Service-Learning, outlines how reflective practice can be facilitated before, during, and after TESOL service-learning experiences. Chapter 5, Learning from Reflections in TESOL Service-Learning, provides various excerpts from authentic reflections on TESOL service-learning experiences to determine what might be learned, especially in terms of academic/cognitive development, professional development, social/civic development, and personal growth. Chapter 6, Impacts of Technology on Reflective Practice in TESOL Service-Learning, details the impact of technology on service-learning and reflective practice, and illustrates with examples of electronic-service-learning projects in various contexts. Chapter 7, Ways Forward in Reflective Practice in TESOL Service-Learning, concludes the book with a consideration of the future of reflective practice in TESOL service-learning contexts.

This book clearly outlines the benefits of service-learning in TESOL contexts by providing an authentic and meaningful learning environment in which to pursue academic outcomes or learning objectives, where participants strive to meet academic objectives *while* engaging in the community service in an equal partnership between the educational institution and the community partner. Such an approach encourages in-depth reflection on the experience and on academic, social, personal, and professional growth and distinguishes service-learning from less reflective types of experiential learning, such as the more traditional field experiences or volunteer work. As such, *Reflective Practice in TESOL Service-Learning* is suitable for preservice and inservice language teachers, language teacher educators and administrators wishing to implement service-learning, certificate students as well as MA and PhD students who want to research service-learning in TESOL contexts, and indeed teachers and teacher educators in different disciplines interested in the concept of service-learning in education.

Thomas S. C. Farrell
Series Editor, *Reflective Practice in Language Education*

Introduction

In Teaching English to Speakers of Other Languages (TESOL) education, reflective practice can foster a disposition of inquiry with a goal of continually improving teaching and learning, yet there is still disagreement about how to define the concept of reflective practice (Farrell, 2019). By exposing the complexities in *Reflective practice in ELT*, Farrell challenges TESOL educators to acknowledge the issues and clarify perceptions in order to improve reflective practice in the future. This challenge is taken up in this book, where issues of reflective practice in the context of TESOL service-learning are explored. Service-learning is "a teaching and learning strategy that integrates meaningful community service with instruction and reflection to enrich the learning experience, teach civic responsibility, and strengthen communities" (National Service-Learning Clearinghouse, cited in Ryan, 2012, p. 4). An essential part of service-learning pedagogy is reflective practice.

To set the foundation for this book, it is helpful to get some insight into what Farrell (2019) discovered from his comprehensive analysis of interpretations and models of reflective practice. He found that, while many teachers claim that they are engaged in reflection (before, during, and after class), there is no common understanding about what reflection means or common language used to discuss it. For example, in his analysis, he identified different forms of reflection from weak to strong. In the weak form of reflection, teachers arbitrarily think about their practice without any particular goal. Conversely, the stronger form is a more deliberate, evidence-based approach to reflection, which involves systematically collecting data, analyzing them in relation to beliefs and practices, and acting on them to improve teaching and learning. It follows that helping preservice English language teachers to strive for this stronger form of reflection would result in more meaningful learning. Beyond this, engaging in a more critical reflection means challenging the ideologies in which practice is embedded. It means questioning norms and injustices and working to transform the world for the better. To promote a common understanding, Farrell (2019) defines reflective practice as:

> A cognitive process accompanied by a set of attitudes in which teachers
> systematically collect data about their practice, and, while engaging in
> dialogue with others, use the data to make informed decisions about
> their practice both inside and outside the classroom. (p. 28)

Interesting parallels exist between the goals of service-learning and the goals of reflective practice, such as constructing meaning, improving teaching and learning, developing self-awareness and a disposition of inquiry, changing understandings, and motivating change. Not surprisingly then, some of the same complexities and issues emerge in both, not least of which is understanding what it is. Multiple interpretations of service-learning and of reflective practice are explored in this book in order to offer TESOL educators and others who implement service-learning in their programs some insight into what reflective practice in TESOL service-learning might look like. In addition, practical tools and strategies are presented to help foster a strong form of reflective practice with pre (or in) service teachers in TESOL service-learning programs. This includes suggestions to help cultivate critical reflections on social justice issues.

Chapter 1 begins by examining what service-learning is and presenting the theoretical foundations of the service-learning context. Its justification and value are outlined before discussing the importance of service-learning in a TESOL context. The value of reflective practice in service-learning is then introduced and parallels to Farrell's (2019) model of reflective practice in ELT are discussed. Finally, challenges and issues in implementing reflective practice in TESOL service-learning contexts are presented to lay the foundation for the rest of the book.

Chapter 2 focuses the discussion of reflective practice in service-learning contexts and, through a series of questions that arise, characterizes reflection in service-learning. Because of the importance of transformative learning in service-learning pedagogy, additional emphasis is placed on critical reflection.

After gaining some insight into the purpose, characteristics, and principles of reflective practice in service-learning explored in Chapter 2, Chapter 3 focuses on analyzing and assessing reflections in TESOL service-learning and the issues associated with this. Goals, outcomes, and objectives in TESOL service-learning are discussed followed by a presentation of several models of reflection analysis. Finally, a sample assessment rubric is presented, not as a prescribed standard, but rather as an example that might inspire ideas for assessing reflections in other TESOL service-learning contexts.

Chapter 4 moves reflection from theoretical concepts and characteristics to applications in practice by suggesting how reflective practice can be facilitated before, during, and after TESOL service-learning experiences. Various artifacts and formats of reflections are discussed and practical tools and strategies are suggested to support the reflection process, such as prompt questions, surveys, observation forms, think aloud protocols (Ericsson & Simon, 1993), quick writes, and models. The chapter concludes with a discussion of the importance of promoting a culture of reflective practice in TESOL service-learning.

Chapter 5 provides a closer look at excerpts from authentic reflections on TESOL service-learning experiences to determine what might be learned from them. They are discussed in relation to the areas of development in service-learning identified in Chapter 2: academic/cognitive development, professional development, social/civic development, and personal growth.

Chapter 6 explores the impact of technology on service-learning and illustrates with examples of electronic-service-learning projects in various contexts. The discussion then moves to a focus on how technology affects reflective practice in service-learning. Benefits and challenges of using technology for reflections are explored. Implications for TESOL service-learning are given and sample guidelines for a multimodal reflection in this context are shared.

The book concludes with a short chapter to consider the future of reflective practice in TESOL service-learning contexts. It is hoped that further discussion, practice, and sharing of research and teaching strategies will advance our understandings of reflective practice in TESOL service-learning contexts.

A FEW COMMENTS ON THE USE OF LANGUAGE IN THIS BOOK

- It is acknowledged that English learner (EL) in some contexts is being replaced with emergent bilingual or multilingual learner or other terms to explicitly reflect an asset orientation towards learning English as an additional language. However, the term EL will be used in this book as it is currently more recognized globally.
- TESOL students are referred to as preservice (ESOL) teachers where applicable.
- To preserve the identity of the preservice teachers quoted, gendered pronouns are replaced by the singular 'they'.
- American spellings are used in this book, except when directly quoting from a British or Canadian source.

Note that IRB approval was granted to collect data and permission to use authentic reflection excerpts was given by the writers.

Chapter 1

What is Service-Learning?

INTRODUCTION

Some educators are more familiar than others with service-learning and the important role that reflective practice plays in it. The purpose of service-learning may also differ according to the context, so it is not surprising that there is considerable variation of interpretations and forms of service-learning. By sharing different interpretations, we can come to a clearer, more informed understanding of what service-learning should or can be. This chapter starts with a discussion of the theoretical foundations and forms of service-learning in general and TESOL service-learning in particular before focusing on reflective practice. It concludes with a consideration of issues in the implementation of reflective practice in TESOL service-learning.

To begin, think about these points for reflection.

Points for Reflection
- Have you heard of service-learning? If yes, what is your understanding of service-learning? If not, what do you think it means?
- Consider how a service-learning approach in TESOL might differ from traditional TESOL approaches.
- Have you ever engaged in service-learning in a TESOL context? If so, what did you learn from the experience?

WHAT IS SERVICE-LEARNING?

Service-learning, used in multiple disciplines at a variety of levels, is a pedagogical approach to teaching and learning that involves community engagement. It is, however, more complex than it appears to be in this definition. Let's consider how the following four definitions use language to emphasize different aspects.

1. The United States National Service-Learning Clearinghouse defines service-learning as "a teaching and learning strategy that integrates meaningful community service with instruction and reflection to enrich the learning experience, civic responsibility, and strengthen communities" (cited in Ryan, 2012, p. 4).
2. Service-learning focuses on "enabling and enhancing student learning through experience, reflection and connection to academic learning" (Brail, 2016, p. 148).
3. Bringle and Clayton (2012) define service-learning as: "a course or competency-based, credit-bearing educational experience in which students (a) participate in mutually identified service activities that benefit the community, and (b) reflect on the service activity in such a way as to gain further understanding of course content, a broader appreciation of the discipline, and an enhanced sense of personal values and civic responsibility" (p. 105).
4. Albanesi et al. (n.d.) summarize service-learning as "a method by which students can learn and develop social and professional competences through active participation in community-oriented experiences that are connected to their academic curricula and provide them with reflective opportunities" (p. 12).

These four definitions are fronted with a focus on learning or education. In other definitions, the community service aspect carries heavier emphasis. For example, in Asia, Ma et al. (2019) interpret service-learning as "a pedagogy that integrates meaningful community service with academic knowledge and skill development. It is an instructional practice providing a self-reflection platform for different stakeholders to enrich their learning experience, nurture civic responsibility, and strengthen community bonding" (p. 3).

Similarly, Europe Engage (https://www.eoslhe.eu/europe-engage/), a service-learning project of a network of European universities, also emphasizes community engagement, citing this definition from McIlrath et al. (2016):

> Service-Learning (sometimes referred to as community based or community engaged learning) is an innovative pedagogical approach that integrates meaningful community service or engagement into the curriculum and offers students academic credit for the learning that derives from active engagement within the community and work on a real-world problem. Reflection and experiential learning strategies underpin the process and the service is linked to the academic discipline. (para. 5)

In European contexts, the priority of service-learning is usually to promote citizenship and civic responsibility and it strives for transformation of knowledge which requires "the integration of civic and social issues, concerns and perspectives with academic content" (Bringle & Clayton, 2020, p. 48). The European Observatory of Service-Learning in Higher Education (EOSLHE https://www.eoslhe.eu/what-we-do/), a space for European universities to network, reflects this view in their website definition and aims:

> Service-learning in higher education is an experiential educational method in which students engage in community service, reflect critically on this experience, and learn from it personally, socially and academically. The activities address human, social and environmental needs from the perspective of social justice and sustainable development, and aim at enriching learning in higher education, fostering civic responsibility and strengthening communities. Service-learning in [sic] is always recognize [sic] with ECTS credits.
>
> It brings together students, academics and the community whereby all become teaching resources, problem solvers and partners. In addition to enhancing academic and real world learning, the overall purpose of [sic] is to instill in students a sense of civic engagement and responsibility and work towards positive social change within society. [Bold type in original removed]

Points for Reflection
- How does your interpretation of service-learning align with those provided (Ryan, 2012; Brail, 2016; Bringle & Clayton, 2012; Albanesi et al., n.d.; Ma et al., 2019 ; Europe Engage, 2016; and EOSLHE, n.d.)?
- Based on these definitions, what do you think are the essential aspects of service-learning pedagogy?
- To what extent do you think teachers should interpret the meaning of service-learning for their contexts?

While interpretations and wording may differ according to local needs and contexts, the commonalities evident in definitions of service-learning seem to be widely accepted. Common essential elements include: academic achievement, a meaningful and mutually beneficial experience, reflection to connect instruction and service, and development of civic responsibility. Other elements, like strengthening of community and positive social change, are also targets.

The proliferation of websites and available resources and guidelines is testament to the popularity of service-learning. For some educators, maybe the allure comes from positive connotations of the name; "service" may give rise to notions of caring and contributing to society, kindness, helpfulness, and goodness. "Learning" suggests purpose, growth, and value. For others, however, the word "service" is considered problematic because of perceptions of a power differential between server and those being served (as in servant and master), or in reference to conscription or national (military) service (Jerome, 2011; Aujla & Hamm, 2018). To avoid misunderstandings in England, the term *citizenship education* (or *active citizenship education*) is sometimes favored over *service-learning* (Jerome, 2011), and in some Canadian contexts, the prominence of the word "service" is lessened by fronting it with the word "community" as in *community service-learning* (Aujla & Hamm, 2018). In other contexts, it can also be referred to as *academic service-learning or community-engaged learning.* Giles (2019) suggests that community engagement is often used as an umbrella term that encompasses service-learning, noting that some people prefer "civic engagement to reflect the political and policy nature of engagement in addition to the community-based work, which is often service" (p. 17).

Points for Reflection
- What do you think of when you hear the word "service"*? Does it have a positive, negative, or neutral connotation for you? How does this connotation impact your view of service-learning?
- To what extent do you think the different language connotations are problematic for service-learning pedagogy?
- Do you think citizenship education and service-learning can/should denote the same thing?
- What institutional structures and supports might be necessary for service-learning to be successful in your context?

*Besides *community service*, consider the many collocations or associations for the word "service", such as national service or military service, teaching service, emergency service, food and beverage service, cleaning service, service staff in a large mansion or estate, religious service, bus service, automobile or appliance service and repair.

SERVICE-LEARNING CONTEXTS

Much of the research in service-learning refers to higher education contexts, but it can be applied in a variety of learning contexts from school settings to adult education settings, which include college and university programs, study abroad programs, and English for Speakers of Other Languages (ESOL) programs. Academic credits may or may not be awarded. In most contexts, service-learning may be a requirement for meeting program outcomes, but in some cases it may be offered as an extra-curricular opportunity. For example, rather than resulting in academic credits or grades, it may be recognized with reduced coursework, bonus points, service-learning points, stamps in an "involvement passport", recognition of service on transcripts, or no incentive except self-gratification and experience gained (Soudy et al., 2015). Projects without academic credit are more typically associated with volunteer work or community service than service-learning, but that does not mean demonstrated learning cannot occur. Indeed, the lack of reward may instill in participants an altruistic commitment to a future of community engagement. There are also community organizations that incorporate service-learning into adult and family learning programs, such as the National Center for Families Learning in the United States (Cramer & Toso, 2015).

Formats of implementation vary from a service-learning experience or project within a course to a dedicated course or program on its own. Experiences can last anywhere from a day to a whole semester or longer. They can be singular (one-off) experiences or sustainable in cycles over time. Needs emerge from the community and, importantly, the experience is jointly organized by the community partner and educational institution. Service-learning experiences can be instructor-led or student-led, and sometimes participants have choices of experiences or options to participate or not.

In Table 1.1, I list a few examples of service-learning projects or experiences that may be suitable in higher education. For more project ideas see Gottlieb and Robinson (2006, p. 48).

Examples of less direct projects are listed in Table 1.2.

Younger participants might engage in service-learning projects, such as those suggested in Table 1.3. For more project ideas see Wang et al. (n.d.), the National Youth Leadership Council website https://www.nylc.org/, and Youth.gov website https://youth.gov/youth-topics/civic-engagement-and-volunteering/service-learning.

Points for Reflection
- Do you have experience with any of these kinds of service-learning projects?
- Do these examples of service-learning projects inspire ideas for projects or partnerships that might work in your context?

Table 1.1. Examples of service-learning experiences in higher education

Service-learning experience	Community partner
Working with refugees in resettlement programs	Resettlement organization, community agency
Helping senior citizens with computer training, or grocery shopping, or other services	Seniors' residence, community agency
Guiding linguistically diverse community members or low-income populations in accessing medical services	Community agency, non-governmental organization (NGO), clinic, hospital
Implementing literacy programs in minority or low-income communities	Local school, community center, literacy center
Working on literacy or job searching skills with former prisoners	Parolee outreach organization, community re-entry agency
Working with vulnerable adolescents	Community youth center, youth agency
Capturing the oral histories of senior citizens	Seniors' residence, long-term care facility
Working on agricultural, animal welfare, or conservation projects	NGO, community agency, local council, international service learning organization
Working on disaster relief projects	NGO, community agency, international service-learning organization

Table 1.2. Examples of less direct service-learning experiences

Service-learning experience	Community partner
Creating welcome packets for immigrants to a community; providing translations	Community agency, resettlement organization
Giving presentations to raise public awareness about an issue	Community center, school, library
Conducting surveys or researching information for a community agency	Community agency
Writing letters and reports; meeting with policy makers to advocate for a needed change	Community agency

Table 1.3. Examples of service-learning projects in K-12 school contexts

Service-learning experience	Community partner
Reading or teaching a lesson on culture to younger peers	School, community center, library
Planting a community garden	Community center, local agency, school
Reading to senior citizens or pre-school children	Local senior citizens residence, nursing home, library, pre-school, community center
Organizing a clothing or toy drive	Local shelter, hospital
Collecting and sorting food donations	Local food bank
Cleaning up the environment	Community agency, conservation organization
Cleaning enclosures or feed rescue animals	Local animal shelter, rescue center

THE PURPOSE OF SERVICE-LEARNING

The rationale for service-learning stems from Dewey (1916), who points out that:

> An ounce of experience is better than a ton of theory simply because it
> is only in experience that any theory has vital and verifiable significance.
> An experience, a very humble experience, is capable of generating and
> carrying any amount of theory (or intellectual content), but a theory
> apart from an experience cannot be definitely grasped even as theory.
> It tends to become a mere verbal formula, a set of catchwords used to
> render thinking, or genuine theorizing, unnecessary and impossible.
> (p. 110)

At risk of oversimplifying Dewey's words, we can learn more through experience than through simple exposure to theory (or intellectual content) in books, lectures, or classwork. Importantly, as Dewey (1910) explains, for learning to take place, experience must involve reflective thinking. It follows that, because service-learning involves practical experience and reflection, it has potential for meaningful learning.

Besides augmenting learning through reflection, service-learning can help develop participants' sense of civic responsibility, and strengthen connections between academic institutions and community partners. These aspects of service-learning are highly valued and have been studied in multiple global contexts (Aujla & Hamm, 2018; Isaacs et al., 2016; Larsen, 2014; Patrick et al., 2019; Roth & Hohn, 2016; Rusu et al., 2015; Tan & Soo, 2020; Tapia, 2012; Wu, 2015).

A CLOSER LOOK AT CIVIC RESPONSIBILITY

Civic responsibility is a key aspect of service-learning that needs elaboration. Gottlieb and Robinson (2006) interpret civic responsibility as "active participation in the public life of a community in an informed, committed, and constructive manner, with a focus on the common good" (p. 16). The goal is to develop mature individuals who think beyond themselves, actively participate in the community around them, and contribute in an informed and beneficial way. Note that, in different contexts, civic responsibility may be known by other terms, such as citizenship education, active citizenship, social justice, public leadership, civic engagement, democratic culture, and these may carry slight differences in emphasis. For example, to emphasize the equal contributions of participants and community partners, service-learning advocates in Argentina prefer the term *solidarity* (Tapia, 2012). Steinberg et al. (2011) use the term *civic mindedness* and define it as "a person's inclination or disposition to be knowledgeable of and involved in the community, and to have a commitment to act upon a sense of responsibility as a member of that community" (p. 20). The Council of Europe (2018), unhappy with the lack of focus and shared understandings of common goals in citizenship education, developed a *Reference framework of competencies for democratic culture*, which guides many service-learning projects in Europe. Twenty competencies are grouped in four areas: values, attitudes, skills, and knowledge and critical understanding. Each area includes competencies that are relevant to TESOL service-learning. For example, in the area of "values", competencies include cultural diversity, democracy, and justice. In "attitudes" competencies include respect, openness, tolerance of ambiguity, and so on. "Skills" include the competencies of critical thinking, listening and observing, empathy, among others. Competencies in "knowledge and critical understanding" include self, language and communication, world history, politics, law, and so on. These competencies set a useful foundation for reflection on civic responsibility, as well as on personal growth and social development.

Two interpretations of effective citizenship in service-learning in England are outlined by Jerome (2011). In one, good citizenship is fostered through engaging in service work in the community. Meeting and building relationships with less advantaged others – with whom students may not otherwise connect – and reflecting on their own position in relation to them, helps promote good citizenship. In another interpretation, the aim is to develop more active citizens by reflecting on sociopolitical issues and questioning policies or governance. This would require more critical reflection on service-learning (see more on critical reflection later in this chapter in response to the question, "What is the difference between reflection and critical reflection?"). Jerome concludes that both interpretations are committed to experiential learning and reflective practice and both can be valued in specific contexts. TESOL service-learning contexts vary as well. Some contexts might require more critical reflections than others, but both could promote meaningful learning. In some contexts, reflections on how academic and professional competencies developed when serving a minority community might suffice, while in other contexts, reflections that critique administrative policies regarding limiting language education, for example, might be appropriate.

Eyler (2002a) supports the second interpretation and cautions that effective citizenship needs more than commitment to serving others; it also requires an ability to analyze problems and to engage in action. This involves constructing knowledge and understanding by observing and making sense of the experience, making connections with prior knowledge and other sources of information, and by developing active skills in asking questions and testing theories. Eyler (2002a), citing earlier work she did with Giles, points out that "theorists have long believed that these capacities are developed through the combination of active engagement and reflection, and recent research demonstrates that reflective, compared to non-reflective, service-learning does have an impact on their development" (2002a, p. 520). She reports on comparisons of cognitive development of students engaged in highly reflective and less reflective service-learning experiences. Those who engaged in more reflection displayed increased ability to systematically frame problems and solutions, analyze complexity, and demonstrate coherent action strategies. Those who reflected less tended to focus on deficiencies and finding the "right answer" to questions. These cognitive abilities are important for developing citizenship and civic responsibility because social issues evident in communities are complex and difficult to identify and solve, and information and perspectives may change and conflict. Reflective citizens are better able to identify issues and navigate the complexities, hence, instructors of service-learning courses that intentionally and systematically facilitate reflective practice are better preparing students for future civic responsibility.

To illustrate, consider individuals volunteering to work at a refugee resettlement organization in their free time. By working with the partner organization and with the refugees themselves, they may learn a little about the refugees, their language or basic needs, and they may feel a sense of gratification for contributing in various ways; but without any formalized reflection activities, they might not explore some of the deeper issues, like how refugees are treated in society, what other challenges they face, why there is a need for resettlement organizations, or how equitable the funding is for such organizations. While the volunteers may think about why the particular refugees came to their community, they may not consider actions that are needed to address the issues. Because "[t]eacher educators are tasked with equipping pre-service teachers (PSTs) to be community-minded, engaged global citizens responsive to the diverse contexts and communities they teach" (Salter & Halbert, 2019, p. 5), more intentional efforts are required to help participants identify and analyze the community problems in all their complexities, and discuss ways to address them. Facilitating critical reflection on service-learning experiences can help participants consider such issues in ways that Eyler (2002a) suggests will help them work towards developing effective citizenship.

Points for Reflection

- John Dewey's (1938) work is almost a century old and, in that time, different approaches to teaching and learning have risen and fallen in popularity; yet, various forms of service-learning, informed by Dewey, continue to be implemented and studied in the United States and elsewhere. Why do you suppose service-learning pedagogy is still popular today and growing worldwide?
- Do you agree with Eyler (2002a) that a commitment to serving others is not enough to demonstrate effective citizenship/civic responsibility? Why or why not?

- How relevant would the European Council's (2018) competencies for democratic culture be for scaffolding civic mindedness in service-learning in your context?
- How might civic responsibility/effective citizenship be linked to TESOL?

SUPPORT FOR SERVICE-LEARNING

Multiple disciplines, such as nursing, social work, education, engineering, technology, and others commonly include service-learning in their programs as an alternative or supplement to traditional approaches (Delano-Oriaran et al., 2015), and this has led to the creation of websites and resources for teachers, as well as service-learning conferences, scholarly journals (such as the *Michigan Journal of Community Service Learning*), research, and service-learning centers and organizations, such as America's National Youth Leadership Council, the European Association of Service-Learning in Higher Education, Asociación De Aprendizaje-Servicio Universitario, and Service-Learning Asia Network (SLAN). Federal funding is often provided for developing and researching service-learning programs (Stewart & Webster, 2011), and, in higher education, multiple universities have their own service-learning or community engagement offices or centers, such as Vanderbilt University's Office of Active Citizenship and Service, Tulane University's Office of Service-learning, Elon University's Center for Engaged Learning, Ngee Ann Polytechnic's Office of Service-Learning, Al Akhawayn University's Office of Community Engagement, to name a few.

Much of the research on service-learning refers to higher education contexts, as mentioned above, but significant contributions have also been made at elementary (primary) and secondary school levels. Citizenship education is part of the school curriculum in England and parts of Europe, and some educators are integrating a service-learning approach to meet the learning requirements (Jerome, 2011; Folgueiras et al., 2019). Prior to 2011, a United States federally funded program called Learn and Serve America supported service-learning for a million young people per year (Ryan, 2012). When budgets were cut in 2011, the program was eliminated but resources continued to be provided by the National Service-Learning Clearinghouse and the National Youth Leadership Council (NYLC https://www.nylc.org). The NYLC's mission is "to create a more just, sustainable, and peaceful world, with young people, their schools, and communities through service-learning". They do this by raising awareness of quality service-learning practice and they developed eight standards to guide service-learning projects in school contexts. They are:

1. Meaningful and personally relevant service.
2. Intentional link to curriculum to meet learning goals or content standards.
3. Ongoing reflection to prompt deep thinking and analysis about oneself and one's relationship to society.
4. Diversity and mutual respect among participants.
5. Youth voice in planning, implementing, and evaluating service-learning experiences with guidance from adults.
6. Mutually beneficial and collaborative partnerships.
7. Ongoing progress monitoring.
8. Appropriate duration and intensity to meet community needs and outcomes. (NYLC, 2008).

Besides developing these standards, NYLC supports a network of members, organizes training and an annual service-learning conference, and shares information about grant opportunities. It provides resources for teachers, such as service-learning handbooks, videos, recommendations, curriculum guides, toolkits, and webinars. The standards and resources not only help educators at multiple levels implement a service-learning approach, they can also prompt new ideas. Youth Service America (n.d.), for example, drew on the NYLC information and standards and developed the IPARD/C model of service-learning to outline the process: Investigation – Preparation & Planning – Action – Reflection – Demonstration/Celebration. This model has been used in multiple contexts. Newman et al. (2015), for example, studied 6,000 middle school students (aged 11–13 years) engaged in service-learning work guided by the IPARD/C model. Results showed improved academic achievement and engagement, civic responsibility, and resiliency.

Other research studies also add support to service-learning pedagogy. For example, in 2011, a meta-analysis of 62 service-learning projects demonstrated that young participants significantly improved their social skills, civic engagement, and academic skills, and increased their attitudes toward self, school, and learning (Celio et al., 2011). Another study of service-learning work at elementary level showed gains for all participants in empathy and community engagement (Scott & Graham, 2015).

Commonalities exist between the National Youth Leadership Council (NYLC) standards for K-12 levels and the Europe Engage quality standards for service-learning in higher education (Stark et al., 2016). Grönlund et al. (2017, p. 6) summarize the 11 quality standards into four essential features of service-learning:

1. Meeting actual community needs so that service-learning meets both real world challenges of the community/relevant community partners and will be meaningful to student participants as well.

2. Service-learning is linked to curriculum, that is to say, relevant to the study program. This requires active involvement of teachers/academic staff, systematic integration in study programs and the option to be recognized for students.

3. Service-learning facilitates active, regular and ongoing student reflection guided by teaching personnel and/or community partners. Reflection should lead to the understanding of diverse perspectives inherent to challenges.

4. The main learning setting in service-learning is located outside the classroom in real world settings of community partners (such as schools, community centers or initiatives).

Information from the service-learning standards, resources, and research studies highlights some common characteristics of service-learning, which we explore next.

COMMON CHARACTERISTICS OF SERVICE-LEARNING

Having different interpretations of service-learning in a wide range of disciplines and contexts can be a good thing. Terry and Bohnenberger (2004) warn against defining service-learning too narrowly as doing so could exclude people and programs, resulting in the loss of "the potential of service-learning to transform both education and our youth" (p. 18). Butin (2011) agrees that the application of service-learning in a plurality of forms and contexts should be embraced in order to better meet local needs, but cautions that it is not a case of "anything goes". It is important to be aware of the varying interpretations in order to come to an informed understanding of what service-learning comprises so that requirements and complexities can be considered relevant to the target context and needs. Though it is sometimes conflated with field experience or teaching practice, service-learning has different requirements and goals.

From my analysis of the literature on service-learning I have found several common requirements of effective service-learning:

1. a strong connection between meeting both academic/learning outcomes and community need
2. equal partnership and increased sense of civic responsibility
3. an emphasis on reflection
4. a goal of transformative learning.

First, it is the learning aspect that distinguishes service-learning from volunteer work. Service-learning provides an authentic and meaningful learning environment in which to pursue academic outcomes or learning objectives. The service-learning experience is carefully and deliberately built into a course or program and therefore integral to achieving success in it. In other words, it is not an "add-on" experience. To this end, participants strive to meet academic objectives *while* engaging in the community service. An important part of this is providing participants with opportunities to make salient connections between academic coursework or theory and the service experience; as mentioned, the service must be purposeful in that it meets an identified community need.

Second, and related to the first, service-learning involves an equal partnership between the educational institution and the community partner, whereby everyone is collaboratively involved in the planning and implementation of the experience, and both sides of the partnership benefit. This means partners must meet before the service-learning begins to discuss needs, goals and objectives, roles, program details, and means of program evaluation. This aspect of equal partnership distinguishes service-learning from teaching practice or internships, where the power differential is typically greater. Importantly, participants from the educational institution need to be trained in what service-learning is and what the expectations are. For example, they should not have the preconceived notion that they are performing a great service to "save" members of the community. Often the partnerships involve different groups that do not ordinarily work together, and these service-learning collaborations offer potential for developing understanding between them. Community partners can benefit from the support and access to resources provided. Concomitantly, participants from the educational institution can build their academic or cognitive skills and learn more about certain community issues and people in the community. An important aspect of this, which should be emphasized, is the increase in civic engagement (Epstein, 2011) and the development of socially responsible citizens (Sturgill & Motley, 2014). By civic engagement, I am referring to community engagement, not political engagement. In a higher education context, cultivating these reciprocal partnerships brings together the institute of higher education and the community in which it is located (Carney, 2004), and a strong relationship between the two is particularly beneficial when universities strive to avoid perceptions of the "ivory tower", supercilious and distant from the realities of everyday community life.

Third, service-learning requires that participants reflect on the experience. The in-depth reflection on the experience and on academic, social, personal, and professional growth distinguishes service-learning from less reflective types of experiential learning, such as field experiences or volunteer work. Indeed, reflection is at the core of service-learning (Barnes & Caprino, 2016; Eyler, 2002b; Jacoby, 2014) and it can take multiple forms, including oral or digital discussion, journal entries, narratives, written papers, blogs, face-to-face or digital presentations, creative works or performances, portfolios, and more. Reflection in service-learning will be discussed in more depth throughout this book.

Finally, a target requirement of service-learning is transformative learning. Traditionally, transformative learning refers to knowledge transformation through which participants raise their awareness of existing practices, challenge their own beliefs, develop their skills, and commit to contributimg to a better world in the future. Typically, this transformation may include the development of practical or professional skills and competencies, greater problem-solving and communication skills, more open-mindedness and empathy, character development, increased sense of civic responsibility and, for some, more clarity of career path.

Transformative learning is also part of critical service-learning which empowers participants to challenge existing assumptions and ideologies more broadly with the goal of viewing their future role as agents of social change (Carrington & Selva, 2010). For example, participants might identify a lack of government funding or support in a school with a high population of minority students as an injustice based on systemic stereotypes. They then think about ways to advocate for social change. The power of this transformative aspect prompted Butin (2011) to suggest moving away from service-learning as a social movement to consider it as an intellectual movement. This is an important goal, but not all service-learning projects include this critical aspect, and it is acknowledged that critical service-learning can sometimes be difficult to achieve within the constraints of an institution. For instance, Jacoby (2014), a proponent of critical service-learning, questions how realistic it is for students to change their perceptions in a short service-learning experience. After a four-week service-learning project, for example, the claim *I now know what it is like to be a refugee* is not very credible. Moreover, in some contexts, it might be detrimental (or even unsafe) to speak or act against the administration. In such cases, however, a distinction could be made between advocating (working for a cause within a system) and activism (working for a cause outside a system). There might be ways to advocate for social change by carefully considering appropriate types of action for the context. This is particularly important in global contexts where service-learning may not be well established and where local traditions are deeply rooted. Van Leeuwen et al. (2017) echo this point in light of their work in community service-learning (CSL) in a Kenyan higher education context:

> researchers and practitioners must incorporate Indigenous perspectives in their work, highlighting the need for CSL [community service-learning] experiences to remain sensitive to historical and contemporary issues, such as those resulting from colonial experiences, along with the various pressures and trends faced by the higher education system as a whole. (p. 130)

Mukuria (2008), also referring to Kenya, reports that political, historical, and cultural conditions, such as the ethnic violence during the 2007 Kenyan elections may have negatively impacted perceptions of community, civic engagement, and the implementation of civic education and service-learning curricula. Similarly, in Morocco, Seilstad (2014) suggests that despite the overall positive results of his service-learning program, some perceptions of civic responsibility may have been negatively affected by incidents of civil unrest. In such contexts, practitioners and community partners may decide it best to introduce the more traditional, less critical forms of service-learning. Transformative learning and social change are possible and ideally should be the goal of service-learning, but service-learning projects must be customized to match local realities and needs.

Points for Reflection

- Does your interpretation of service-learning encompass the four requirements outlined here: strong connection between meeting both academic outcomes and community need, equal partnership and increased sense of civic responsibility, emphasis on reflection, and goal of transformative learning? If not, how and why does it differ?
- Consider your program outcomes and/or course curriculum and identify the knowledge, skills, and dispositions that could be developed by integrating a service-learning approach.
- In your context, would you advocate for a traditional or critical form of service-learning? Why?

SERVICE-LEARNING AROUND THE WORLD

Service-learning is growing globally and I would like to highlight some of work that is being done in different countries around the world. While it is not feasible to discuss all regions and programs, several examples are highlighted here and illustrated with selected details.

North America

In the United States, service-learning is well established, and much of the literature on service-learning is based on 50 years of work in US contexts. For examples, see the *Michigan Journal of Community Service-Learning* https://quod.lib.umich.edu/cgi/t/text/text-idx?page=issues;c=mjcsl;c=mjcsloa;g=mjcslg;xc=1 or multiple websites, like Youth.gov https://youth.gov/youth-topics/civic-engagement-and-volunteering/service-learning.

In Canada service-learning has been spreading for more than two decades, drawing much from American service-learning models (Aujla & Hamm, 2018). As in the US, both traditional and more critical approaches are taken in Canada. In fact, Chambers (2009) conceptualized a continuum of overlapping approaches to service-learning in Canada along which he identified three salient points: *philanthropic* approaches, *social justice* approaches, and *social transformation* approaches. *Philanthropic* approaches are the traditional forms of service-learning in which participants work to meet a community need and academic objectives. Here, changes in mindset and beliefs occur through reflecting on the experience. *Social justice* approaches do this as well, but participants delve deeper into the social causes of particular challenges for the specific community participants that they work with, and they consider ways to support them. The *social transformation* approach builds on the first two, but participants analyze broader, more systemic issues beyond the immediate context and consider how to bring about wider social change. An example of the social justice approach is published by Grekul et al. (2018), and an example of the social transformation approach is clear in the work of Martin and Pirbhai-Illich (2015), who assert that more critical approaches are needed in order to change systemic inequities.

Most community service-learning in Canadian higher education settings is implemented in academic courses, but extra-curricular service-learning experiences are also evident (Taylor et al., 2015). In all, community-service-learning exists at 50 or more post-secondary institutions in Canada (Kahlke & Taylor, 2018), but it is not federally mandated, there is no national agenda for service-learning, and funding is limited. To illustrate, the Canadian Alliance for Community-Service-Learning (CACSL https://mcconnellfoundation.ca/grant/canadian-alliance-for-community-service-learning-cacsl/), a network of faculty and post-secondary professionals who support community service-learning, was set up in 2004 with grant funding. After the funding stopped, CACSL was dissolved, though some smaller, regional networks seem to be emerging.

Asia

In Asia, service-learning is well known in several countries and in 2004, various post-secondary institutions set up a Service-Learning Asia Network (SLAN, http://su.edu.ph/slan/) for members to "share ideas about the development of service-learning in the region and have united together to encourage cross-national collaborations". By 2020 the secretariat duties of Asia SLAN were being managed by Silliman University Office of Community Engagement and service-learning, Philippines. The network convenes an annual Asia Pacific Regional Conference on Service-Learning and highlights various publications that outline service-learning work that is being done in Asia. At the National Institute of Education Singapore, service-learning is well established with strong government support. In 2009, Goh et al. published a book reporting on successful Group Endeavours in Service-Learning (GESL) projects. GESL is a student-led service-learning program, required for graduation, in which groups of 16–20 preservice teachers work together with a local partner to meet a community need. Eleven years after the publication of the book, Tan and Soo's (2020) findings from interviews of preservice teachers engaged in the GESL program suggest that the program continues to be effective in developing self-awareness, understanding of community needs, increased communication, and collaboration skills. In Malaysia, Sandaran (2012) writes a compelling explanation to convince readers why service-learning could be beneficial for building sustainable community partnerships and developing socially responsible citizens, and in other Asian examples, Murtiningsih (2015) describes how service-learning projects in TESOL undergraduate programs in Indonesia help prepare preservice English language teachers there. Other examples describe projects in China (Lu et al., 2019), Hong Kong (Au Yeung et al., 2019), Philippines (Uy, 2019), and Taiwan (Wu, 2015; Wu, 2018). With some exceptions, much of the literature on service-learning in Asia is fairly recent and shows positive outcomes.

Europe

In 2019, the European Observatory of Service-Learning in Higher Education (EOSLHE) was formed to support service-learning amongst members of the European network Europe Engage. Members collaboratively provide multiple resources, track service-learning experiences, promote engaged citizenship in Europe, and foster relevant scholarly activities. Data from the 2021 annual report (Ribeiro et al., 2021) reveal that, to date, 104 experiences from 19 European countries have been shared. "In addition to increasing the civic engagement, innovative teaching approaches like SL are seen as well to contribute to reducing the current high-level skills gap between students and labour market needs" (Albanesi et al. n.d., p. 18). That said, considerable variability in interpreting and implementing service-learning exists across the continent. For example, in Germany service-learning programs can be found in 64 universities, while some universities display little understanding of the relevance of community engagement (Roth & Hohn, 2016). Service-learning programs in Spain exist in 24 universities, yet only six have implemented formal service-learning policies (Opazo et al., 2016; Ruiz-Ordonez et al., 2020). Evidence of service-learning in Romania is found in a published study by Rusu et al. (2015) who report on preservice teachers' engagement in online ESL tutoring. They found a positive correlation between engagement in service-learning and grade point averages (GPAs). England has mandatory citizenship education, and to promote active participation, critical awareness, and community engagement with equal partners, there have been calls to integrate more service-learning into the curricula in England (Asghar & Rowe, 2017; Birdwell et al., 2013).

Australia and New Zealand

An example of service-learning pedagogy in Australia and New Zealand is Yang's (2015) study of an English teaching and learning experience involving Australian TESOL student teachers and international refugees. Results show that participants developed greater intercultural competence, language teaching skills, and cultural knowledge, while refugees reduced their culture shock, improved their English, and learned problem-solving skills. Notwithstanding this success, interpretations of service-learning in Australia vary widely, with many equating it with a form of work-integrated learning (Patrick et al., 2019). Advocacy for service-learning with a focus on inclusive education and engagement with community is growing, however, and, in 2019, a service-learning network and summit took place at Griffith University. Hobart, and William Smith Colleges in New Zealand, in cooperation with the University of Auckland, offer a service-learning program for juniors and seniors, which includes courses in Maori language and culture, ecology and conservation, community arts, and Laban movement analysis. Multiple study-abroad service-learning projects are also available in Australia and New Zealand, though they may or may not align with all the characteristics or standards of service-learning outlined earlier.

Central and South America

In Central and South America, service-learning is less well known in the literature. Calvert and Valladares Montemayor (2018) point out that, in Mexico, the constitution mandates a minimum of 480 hours of community service for all undergraduate degrees, but international awareness of programs there is not usually accessible in English, or "professors researching the impact and processes do not typically publish in journals due to restrictive publication practices" (p. 52). There has been some interesting work reported in Argentina with digital technologies in secondary school service-learning projects in which information and communication technologies were found to help make the learning more visible (Tapia Sasot, 2020). In addition, in Trinidad and Tobago, McDonald (2012) describes assessment in a successful service-learning course comprising students from Business Management, Human Resource Management, Accounting, and Nursing.

Sub-Saharan Africa

Service-learning and civic education also exist in Africa, though research is limited (Van Leeuwen et al., 2017). The Association of International Schools in Africa (AISA) produced a 2016 handbook for service-learning that is available online for school teachers and the public, but most published literature focuses on service-learning in higher education. Notably in South Africa, Isaacs et al. (2016) report on a critical service-learning project in which psychology students worked with a local organization in a fishing community north of Cape Town to provide a series of workshops to support adolescents and families. From the experience, the students developed greater introspection and community awareness and they were able to identify systemic injustices like language barriers and lack of facilities and support. McMillan and Stanton (2014) report on a study-abroad service-learning program organized by Stanford University's Bing Overseas Studies Program in Cape Town. The program was carefully planned so as not to become a kind of tourism. Students worked with a variety of community organizations and the work focused on the importance of partnerships in terms of who is serving whom.

Arabic-Speaking Countries

Kassabgy and Salah El-Din (2013) report positive results from service-learning in which Arabic-speaking students in an undergraduate TEFL (Teaching English as a Foreign Language) course taught English to Arabic-speaking custodians, security guards, and housekeeping staff at the American University of Cairo. Their findings show increases in self-awareness, civic responsibility, and empathy in addition to the development of leadership and communication skills. Seilstad (2014) has pointed out that service-learning is rare in Arabic-speaking countries, but starting to appear in curricula and in extra-curricular contexts – though it typically does not take priority. That said, he reports on a promising study at Al Akhawayn University in Morocco where service-learning is encouraged in the university's strategic plan of 2010–2014 and where students are required to complete 60 hours of community service for graduation. Seilstad found academic, personal, social, and civic gains in an English teaching service-learning project, but, to confirm these results, he has called for more work to be done in Arabic-speaking contexts. In response, Suwaed (2018) studied a service-learning project in Libya in which undergraduates in the English language department at Sabratha College of Arts taught English to low-income members of the local community. She found value in the program with benefits in the development of knowledge, skills, self-awareness, and citizenship commitment to community engagement. In Qatar, Soudy et al. (2015) report on a successful service-learning program in which university students implemented an English literacy program for migrant workers.

Israel

In Israel, Lahav et al. (2018) report favorable findings of a five-year study of service-learning experiences in an occupational therapy program.

This glimpse into a number of service-learning experiences around the world shows how approaches, challenges, and outcomes can vary due to different interpretations of service-learning and the context in which it is embedded. Despite the differences, however, the goals of service-learning are shared, and learning about other's work can inform our own.

Points for Reflection

- Consider the advantages and disadvantages of the following service-learning scenarios:
  - implementing a service-learning project prescribed by a central authority (i.e., project structure, methods, expected results designed by the administration)
  - designing and implementing a service-learning project on your own with your choice of community partner
  - developing and implementing a service-learning project in collaboration with colleagues, students, and community organizations.
- Which of the above scenarios would best fit your context? Which would you prefer to be involved in and why?
- How would you feel about student-led service-learning projects rather than instructor-led projects?

STUDY ABROAD AS SERVICE-LEARNING

In addition to local service-learning programs around the world, several non-governmental, as well as commercial, organizations offer programs that send students to various international destinations for service-learning experiences. An American organization called the International Partnerships for Service-Learning and Leadership (IPSL) interprets service-learning as "a pedagogy that links academic study with practical experience of volunteer community service to make the study immediate, applicable, and relevant through knowledge, analysis, and reflection" (Dubinsky et al., 2012, p. 156). IPSL provides opportunities for students to experience community engagement in another country and take courses there in language, culture, history, advocacy, ecology, and more. Students complete coursework and community service and engage in reflection activities, such as journal writing and essays, as well as paired and group discussions. Since its origin in 1992, the ethos of IPSL has changed and it has launched a program called Community Organizing and Social Activism (COSA https://www.ipsl.org/cosa), which adopts a more critical service-learning approach. This can raise questions about the feasibility of activism in countries where such action may be resisted or even dangerous, but they point out on their website that "peaceful social movements are highly successful in creating change worldwide".

Van Auken (2019) of Volunteer Forever provides information about other study-abroad service-learning organizations, such as Global Vision International (https://www.gviusa.com/international-service-learning/), Global Leadership Adventures (https://www.experiencegla.com/), International Volunteer HQ (https://www.volunteerhq.org/service-learning-abroad/), and Maximo Nivel (https://maximonivel.com/tefl-tesol/). Other study-abroad organizations include International Service-Learning (https://islonline.org/), and Amizade (https://amizade.org/), which has recently added virtual service-learning programs.

The study-abroad organizations identified here are just a few of many. For individuals considering an external organization offering service-learning through study abroad programs, it is important to match the program with the desired purpose and requirements and then determine how reputable the companies or organizations are. Another important consideration is the kind of reflective practice used and the ways it is implemented and monitored.

Points for Reflection

- What do you think could be the benefits of people engaging in service-learning in a country other than their own?
- What resources and connections do you or your institution have to assist students in gaining access to local and international communities?
- How might technology be used to facilitate international service-learning experiences when there are restrictions on travel?

BENEFITS OF SERVICE-LEARNING

With the development and spread of service-learning generally, more has become known about the benefits and the issues. Research results on the effectiveness of service-learning have been mixed, but when designed effectively, service-learning has been shown to improve teaching and learning (Eyler, 2002a, b; Garver et al., 2018; Newman et al., 2015; Rodríguez-Izquierdo, 2021; Scott & Graham, 2015). This claim, regarding police officer training, clearly demonstrates the benefit of community engagement, which distinguishes service-learning from traditional classroom approaches to learning:

> Service-learning opportunities in college provide future police officers a chance to develop civic engagement skills. It also gives them the chance to get to know the communities they will police. Among students who participated in a criminal justice service-learning course working with young people in the community, 80% reported a change from stereotypical assumptions that all of them would be criminals to a better understanding of them as individuals with goals and potential – some not so different from the students' own dreams. Almost 90% said they had come to understand the community, which they believed would serve them in their criminal justice careers. (Bouffard, 2020)

Many of the research studies conclude that service-learning can be effective if it is well planned and organized. For example, Taylor et al. (2015) echo Martin and Pirbhai-Illich's (2015) work when they refer to community service-learning experiences in Canada, cautiously claiming that it can promote critical thinking and civic responsibility, "if they are carefully organized, have clarity of purpose, are relevant to students' professional futures, address the emotional dimensions of students' learning, and provide opportunities for ongoing student reflections, guided by faculty who understand students' levels of understanding about social problems" (p. 19). That said, work still needs to be done to promote a deeper understanding of service-learning and its effectiveness in different contexts, as well as to promote a more critical service-learning pedagogy where appropriate (Stewart & Webster, 2011).

IMPORTANCE OF SERVICE-LEARNING IN TESOL PROGRAMS

While research on service-learning is not new, especially in US contexts, applications in the area of TESOL are not so well known in the literature (Wurr, 2018). English language teachers, especially those in English as a second language (ESL) contexts, often work with disenfranchised communities that have various needs, for example, English learners (ELs) in under-resourced schools, refugees, and linguistically diverse adult immigrants who need access to services; hence, service-learning pedagogy is a natural fit in TESOL education programs. Service-learning in TESOL is valuable because it enables higher education institutions and their community partners to collaborate in implementing projects that benefit both preservice teachers and culturally and linguistically diverse learners. Indeed Purmensky

(2009) claims that, for TESOL preservice teachers, "[s]ervice-learning projects address academic, cultural, pedagogical, self-reflective, educational, and diversity issues all through one pedagogically sound project" (p. 19). Burke et al. (2021) identify multiple benefits for preservice ESOL teachers including: the development of English language teaching (ELT) skills, greater ability to connect theory and practice, first-hand experience of the stages of second language acquisition, exposure to a variety of teaching strategies and resources, and an opportunity to become part of the school community. The ELs benefit from the additional English support and personal attention. The focus of this book is on projects that entail ELT but, as mentioned, service-learning in TESOL may also consist of related activities, like resettlement programs, social activities, or cultural projects.

Points for Reflection
- What needs might a school with a high population of English learners have that service-learning could address?
- Besides English language teaching, are there other kinds of service projects that TESOL service-learning programs might provide in your communities or context?
- How might community service-learning that does not directly involve teaching benefit TESOL preservice teachers and their community partners?

Carrington and Selva (2010) point out that "[P]re-service teachers often enter teacher education programs with problematic or unexamined assumptions, beliefs and knowledge about students, teaching and the role of schools in society" (p. 46). In the field of TESOL, these issues can be even more apparent. While students enter a TESOL program with a range of life experiences, many speakers of English as a first language have little or no experience in foreign language classrooms and frequently lack experience in working with culturally and linguistically diverse learners. Incorporating meaningful service-learning into TESOL programs can help to address these limitations as it provides opportunities to raise preservice teachers' awareness of issues in teaching English to diverse learners and helps them improve their skills through increased opportunities to practice and reflect on their language teaching and related issues.

Potential benefits for preservice teachers can include academic or cognitive growth, personal growth, social growth, and career growth (Macknish et al., 2018). These growth areas include improved ability to connect theory and practice, greater empathy, cultural and linguistic sensitivity, improved intercultural communication skills and English language instructional strategies, as well as validation of chosen career (Fitts & Gross, 2012; Purmensky, 2009; Schneider, 2019; Wurr, 2018). Atkinson Smolen et al. (2013) found that preservice teachers in a TESOL service-learning program serving Karen refugees increased their academic knowledge, as well as their professional and personal development in terms of cultural understanding, civic engagement, and commitment. In discussing how service-learning enriched an MA TESOL course, Tomaš et al. (2017) conclude "that service-learning pedagogy is a viable tool in reconceptualizing TESOL methods and materials courses in ways that help reinforce theory-practice connections" (p. 64). Similarly, Suwaed (2018) found that preservice teachers in Libya improved their understanding of lesson planning and teaching with classroom materials. Interestingly, they also found that "their ideas about teaching and assessment were challenged" (p. 36). Findings in a study by Wu (2018) of preservice Taiwanese teachers teaching in the Philippines showed increased knowledge and skills in developing language proficiency, as well as cultural awareness. Similarly, Cho and Gulley (2017) reveal how service-learning contributed to developing TESOL graduate students' intercultural awareness, civic responsibility, and teacher identity. They also found that it helps students bridge theory and practice, as well as "expand their comfort zones in dealing with diversity and reflect on their own social positions in relation to others" (p. 631). In another study in Taiwan, Wu (2015) found transformed perceptions and personal and professional growth. Kassabgy and Salah El-Din (2013) also found positive results in terms of development of civic responsibility in an EFL setting in Egypt. Hill-Jackson and Lewis (2011) add that learning about civic engagement is significant because teachers need to know how to make connections between school and community.

The community partner should also benefit from service-learning. Service-learning programs can help meet needs of ELs in many schools and of language minority adults in various contexts by providing (additional) linguistic and social support, which can involve formal language and culture classes, individual or small group tutoring, language partnerships, after-school clubs, family literacy programs, or other activities. Wu and Dahlgren (2011) claim that service-learning helps immigrants to overcome language barriers and social problems. Other benefits can include improved academic success, increased confidence, motivation to learn, more positive attitudes toward writing, and sense of community (Macknish et al., 2018; Diversi & Mecham, 2005). The positive findings for both preservice teachers and community partners from these and other studies build support for TESOL service-learning.

From a critical perspective, service-learning work with "culturally and linguistically diverse students not only helps to promote diversity but also advances educational equity" (Weah et al., cited in Wu & Dahlgren, 2011, p. 263). When working with refugees or immigrant students, particularly those of low socioeconomic backgrounds or in schools or communities where these students are marginalized or where resources are limited, service-learning projects provide structured opportunities for the learners to get support and for the preservice teachers to gain first-hand experience working with diverse groups. By engaging with learners from marginalized communities, preservice teachers can gain insight into the social realities of these groups and the challenges they face related to racial and linguistic injustices, like lack of funding and/or other support. The goal is for preservice teachers to build empathy and question existing assumptions and ideologies. Hill-Jackson and Lewis (2011), for example, suggest that service-learning programs in multicultural settings have the potential to help white preservice English language teachers understand their privileged position and promote social justice. Similarly, in Qatar, Soudy et al. (2015) found that awareness of privileged positions was raised: "the program helps students develop personal, social, and citizenship skills. Students develop empathy for, and build bridges with this population, while appreciating their diverse community and their privileged lives" (p. 359). To achieve this, TESOL education programs must focus on training preservice teachers, not only to develop their professional language teaching skills, but also to become advocates for these marginalized groups (Wu & Dahlgren, 2011).

In summary, the benefits of well-designed service-learning experiences for preservice ESOL teachers can include:

- increased awareness of academic and pedagogical issues
- development of ELT skills and strategies
- understanding and reinforcement of theory–practice connections
- improved skills in reflection and critical thinking
- enhanced self-awareness and sense of personal and professional identity
- greater cultural and linguistic awareness and empathy
- increased awareness of diversity and social justice issues
- development of experience and confidence working with culturally and linguistically diverse learners
- validation of career choices
- improved citizenship skills and sense of civic responsibility
- greater community engagement and understanding.

Benefits for community partners and multilingual learners can include:

- additional linguistic support
- additional social support
- improved academic success
- increased confidence
- stronger motivation and positive attitude toward language learning
- increased sense of community.

To attain benefits or positive outcomes of service-learning in a TESOL context – whether related to academic growth, civic responsibility, career growth, social growth, personal growth, or pursuit of social justice – service-learning projects must be carefully planned and implemented and evidence of the effectiveness of service-learning needs to be elicited through reflective practice.

> **Points for Reflection**
> - How might the benefits of a TESOL service-learning experience differ from the benefits of a traditional TESOL course?
> - How might engaging in TESOL service-learning help preservice ESOL teachers become more culturally sensitive?
> - What might convince you, or a stakeholder, that a TESOL service-learning experience is effective?

THE VALUE OF REFLECTIVE PRACTICE IN SERVICE-LEARNING

As Dewey (1916) points out, "No experience having a meaning is possible without some element of thought" (p. 169). If we equate meaningful experience with learning, and thought with reflection, this means that we don't learn from the experience; rather we learn from reflecting on the experience. For this reason, engaging in reflective practice is an essential part of service-learning. Stewart (2011) makes the point that reflection in service-learning is what links the academic work to the community experience, where reflection is generally "understood to be deliberative practice of thinking about past experiences or knowledge in order to make meaning, enable better choices or actions, or increase effectiveness in future attempts" (pp. 38–39). Brail (2016) highlights the importance of reflective practice in service-learning when she argues that "higher grade achievement is also largely irrelevant from a learning perspective if it does not also go hand in hand with students' abilities to develop deep connections through critical and *reflective* [my emphasis] experience alongside connection and relevance to service-learning partners" (p. 156). It is through reflection that participants can demonstrate their ability to connect theory and practice, display a sense of inquiry and knowledge of existing practices, connect personal and interpersonal development, explore beliefs, identify issues, challenge assumptions, consider action, show self-awareness, metacognition, and learning progress, and display critical thinking and transformational learning.

Interesting parallels exist between reflective practice in service-learning and reflective practice in ELT. Farrell's (2015, 2019) model of reflective practice includes five stages or levels, namely *philosophy*, *principles*, *theory*, *practice*, and *beyond practice*. The stages are connected but it is not necessary to follow them in a prescribed sequence. Each stage is explored below as it aligns to service-learning.

The first stage of reflection in Farrell's model is *philosophy*. By *philosophy* he is referring to the teacher's outlook, which is based on their identity both in and out of the classroom. This *philosophy* has been shaped since birth by socioeconomic background, ethnicity, family, and personal values. Reflecting on *philosophy* requires that teachers examine who they are and how they got to where they are. Such an examination gives insight into a teacher's identity and allows them to reflect at the next level. In service-learning, this is illustrated in a study of white preservice teachers in a program with multicultural learners. Hill-Jackson and Lewis (2011) found that they needed to insist that preservice teachers reflect on their positions of privilege, race, and multicultural ideals in order to understand the experience. They claim that a preservice teacher "who has an unexamined positionality, uncommitted emotional investments, and poor reflection in the service-learning field is, at best, service loitering" (p. 311). In other words, for meaningful learning to take place, participants in service-learning must be self-aware and consider how their position may not be neutral. Once participants understand their *philosophy*, they can move on to explore their beliefs about teaching and learning.

The second stage of Farrell's (2019) model is *principles* of reflection. Here he means "the teachers' assumptions, beliefs, and conceptions about teaching and learning" (p. 51). *Principles* are closely linked to *philosophy* as beliefs, too, are shaped by an individual's background. Reflecting on beliefs is important because it can reveal why teachers do what they do in terms of instructional decisions and actions. For example, if a teacher, in her own education, was taught prescriptive grammar, she may believe that it is important to do the same in her English language teaching. She may find, however, that teaching prescriptive grammar leads to disengagement of the ELs that she teaches, causing her to question her beliefs. Reflecting on *principles* is important in a service-learning context as well. The purpose is to push participants out of their comfort zones and compel them to examine their personal beliefs about teaching and learning – specifically through service-learning – as well as their beliefs about working with diverse learners. It can be difficult to change lifelong beliefs or attitudes that may interfere with service-learning or working with diverse learners, so in a TESOL context, it can help to plan effective service-learning experiences with opportunities for preservice teachers to observe and engage with diverse learners. Increased exposure provides more information, perspectives, and practical experience for preservice teachers to reflect on. Thinking about the experience in conjunction with their *philosophy*, and determining why something worked or failed in a particular context makes the reflection deeper and more meaningful for their professional development. Indeed, Maddux and Donnett (2015) point out that for learning to occur in service-learning, a reevaluation of assumptions is necessary, resulting in a conclusion that can be applied in future experiences.

Reflecting on *philosophy* and *principles* informs *theory,* which is the third stage of Farrell's (2019) model. He makes the point that language teachers reflect on *theory* learned in teacher education courses, but they also construct their own *theory* of practice. It is important for teachers to reflect on *theory* because it informs their planning. Connecting theory and practice applies to service-learning, too, where linking academic learning (theory) and community experience (practice) is a crucial part of the approach. Because one of the key aspects of service-learning is meeting academic outcomes through community engagement, demonstrating understanding of theory–practice links in reflection is expected and "[t]he quality of the reflection activity impacts the academic outcomes associated with service-learning" (Hullender et al., 2015, p. 61). In other words, if participants are not able to effectively connect theory and practice, they may struggle to meet the academic outcomes. More importantly, they may not have insight into why what they do is, or is not, effective.

Reflecting on *practice* in ELT, the next stage in Farrell's (2019) model, involves examining teaching and learning. Building on Schön (1983, 1987), Farrell expands reflection-in-action and reflection-on-action to include reflection-for-action. During a lesson, teachers reflect-in-action by considering why something is happening and responding to it on the spot. For example, if a teacher observes an EL struggling with some lexis and she realizes that it is because the language is idiomatic, she may immediately explain that the meaning is not literal and provide a synonym or paraphrase for the EL. After a lesson, teachers reflect-on-action by examining occurrences in retrospect, which enables them to question why something happened and what could have happened differently. It is not necessarily about solving problems; it could be about confirming positive actions or simply exploring alternatives. Considering the previous example, the teacher may think about the proficiency level of the class and the level of the text provided and decide that it was fine to expose the EL to the new language and clarify on the spot. Alternatively, she may decide the text was too difficult, or that she did not pre-teach enough vocabulary, or that the specific EL was not yet at the same proficiency level as their classmates. Before a subsequent lesson, teachers reflect-for-action by using their knowledge and experience to anticipate events that may happen and consider in advance different ways to address them. In the same example, the teacher may decide that next time, she needs to use a different text, or provide a glossary, or supplementary support for that EL, or teach a lesson on idiomatic language. Using an asset, rather than deficit approach, the teacher might even plan a cultural exchange, where ELs teach each other idioms from their home languages. She may also look at herself with a self-critical lens and decide that she needs to do some scholarly reading or enroll in some professional development training regarding vocabulary teaching or selecting appropriate texts. Reflecting on *practice* plays a big role in service-learning reflection also, and, like Farrell, service-learning scholars advocate pre, during, and post-service phases of reflection (Eyler et al., 1996; Stewart, 2011). It is through reflection on *practice* that participants develop an enhanced understanding of practice, make sense of their service-learning experience, and develop meaning from it that they might apply in future.

The last stage in Farrell's (2019) model is reflecting *beyond practice*, which refers to critical reflection on relevant sociopolitical and affective/moral issues influencing language teaching and learning. For example, in the scenario above, the teacher may conclude that the issue is more widespread and decide to advocate for ELs by starting an awareness campaign to inform her colleagues about the challenges that ELs face regarding (idiomatic) language use. She might provide her colleagues with some strategies on how to support ELs in their classes, or she may implement workshops for them on how to design tests that are free of unnecessarily complex or culturally biased language. In other contexts, teachers may question the need to teach from required texts or follow curricula dictated by administration if it does not seem relevant or authentic. Multiple service-learning scholars advocate such critical reflection in service learning as it is here that personal growth and transformational learning becomes most evident. Hullender et al. (2015), for instance, claim that "[t]ransformative learning, often linked as an outcome of a well-designed service-learning experience, signifies a dramatic change in knowledge, skills, and how we understand our relationship to the world around us" (p. 74). Similarly, Maddux and Donnett (2015) point out that reflections that demonstrate explicit connections between participants' individual experiences in a service-learning context and the broader "superstructure of their understanding of the world" (p. 67) will help them to clarify problematic situations. If it is appropriate, participants can be encouraged to reflect on current practices and ideologies and challenge them in light of social justice. For example, participants might question the prevailing assumptions or norms perpetuated in an institution, stereotyping of race and ethnicity, lack of inclusion, lack of funding or resources for minorities, or other issues. They can then consider ways that they might contribute to a more socially just world and "reconstruct their own vision of what their future role as a teacher could be" (Carrington & Selva, 2010, p. 54).

Farrell (2019) characterizes reflective practice as "a focus, not only on the intellectual, cognitive and metacognitive aspects of practice, but also the spiritual, moral and emotional non-cognitive aspects that acknowledge the inner life of teachers" (p. 27). This is mirrored in service-learning approaches that suggest embracing the emotional aspect of reflection (Thompson & Pascal, 2012), rather than the traditional service-learning approaches that recommended standing back and reflecting in an objective manner. Stewart's (2011) element of introspection in service-learning advocates "reintegrating interiority, spirituality, soul, and unique personal ways of being into service-learning and community engagement" (p. 60) in unison with external approaches in order to create a multilayered approach to service-learning that acknowledges different learning styles of students. Logic suggests that drawing on emotion and spirituality would enable more personal and sincere reflection, which can make the experience more meaningful. Indeed, I have found it valuable for learning when participants in service-learning reveal their joys and frustrations in their reflections on their experiences, as these can then be explored for causes and impacts, which can inform future practice.

Points for Reflection

- Identify a service-learning (or ELT) experience that you have had and reflect on it by systematically considering each stage of Farrell's (2019) model: *philosophy, principles, theory, practice, beyond practice.*
- To what extent do you believe that critical reflection and transformative learning are important in TESOL service-learning?
- What role do you think emotion plays (or should play) in reflective practice in TESOL service-learning contexts?

In addition to his new model of reflective practice, Farrell (2019) has identified six principles of reflective practice in English language teaching (ELT), which can also be used to guide reflective practice in service-learning: reflective practice is holistic; reflective practice is evidence-based; reflective practice involves dialogue; reflective practice bridges principles and practices; reflective practice requires a disposition to inquiry; reflective practice is a way of life. These principles are discussed in Chapter 2 as they apply to reflective practice in service-learning.

CHALLENGES AND ISSUES REGARDING REFLECTIVE PRACTICE IN TESOL SERVICE-LEARNING

Reflective practice in TESOL service-learning contexts is not without challenges and issues. These challenges start from a lack of understanding of concepts. Multiple interpretations of service-learning and of reflective practice can result in a mismatch of expectations and behavior between participants and educators, which can lead to an unsuccessful result. Clarity and shared understandings obviously need to exist between educators and participants. It goes without saying that, in order to foster reflective practice in service-learning, educators must first be familiar with reflective practice themselves and then they need to be able to communicate the purpose and their expectations to participants so that there are shared understandings. Without a shared understanding, the reflections are not meaningful tools for learning. For example, my own reviews of reflections on service-learning show that some preservice teachers do not understand the personal and contextualized nature of reflection (or for that matter the contextualized nature of service-learning and of ELT). They are looking for models of the "right" way to reflect (and teach). Herein lie some dilemmas. If educators outline expectations in detail, then reflecting on experience may become a prescribed exercise rather than an individualized, personal, and meaningful approach for learning. Stewart (2011) claims that reflection can become a mindless, product-oriented task rather than a process-oriented task for continuous learning over time and contexts. The risk is that reflection can then "straight jacket" learning and be reduced to a management tool (Stewart, 2011, p. 41) to steer the service-learning project. Farrell (2019) makes a related point that, sometimes in ELT, reflections can become problem-solving tools. The consequence of this is that the (preservice) teacher's role is reduced to that of technician conducting mechanical reflections to diagnose and solve problems in the classroom.

There are common, practical challenges in fostering reflective practice in service-learning, too. Often there is insufficient time for reflection or for teaching effective reflective practice. This is particularly true as preservice teachers enter programs with varying levels of familiarity with service-learning, with teaching, with working with diverse learners, and with skills in reflective practice (Jaeger, 2013). Time is therefore needed to evaluate preservice teachers' understandings and skill levels and from that determine how to "teach" or foster reflection with different individuals. This raises another issue. Is it even possible to teach someone how to reflect? Effective reflection requires a sense of self-awareness and a disposition of inquiry, but some may question if it is possible to "teach" a disposition (this is discussed in Chapter 4).

Assuming that there are shared understandings of the purpose and expectations of reflective practice in service-learning, and that there is sufficient time for multiple opportunities to facilitate reflective practice, there may be a risk that the repetition and routine acts of reflection can lead to mindlessness, or boredom (Stewart, 2011). Many preservice teachers may be overwhelmed and fatigued with their day-to-day studies and service-learning workload, where meeting the immediate needs of the learners is their focus. They may not have time or inclination to engage in any kind of deliberate reflection. Indeed, they may just want to "turn off" rather than keep thinking about their day. Similarly, Farrell (2019) cautions that "burn-out" can occur if teachers engage in intensive reflections every day. An added issue here for reflective practice in service-learning is that "reflection fatigue" may cause preservice teachers to think negatively about the service-learning experience, such that they decide not to implement service-learning in their future teaching or engage in community service as a future citizen.

Possibly the most common issues that emerge in reflections involve a lack of depth or focus. In my experience, I have seen reflections on service-learning that lack evidence or details to support claims, or reflections that are entirely superficial and could be considered simply as descriptive play-by-plays of the experience with no reflective or critical thought at all. Other reflections reveal that preservice teachers fail to find or articulate connections between theory and practice, or they may display too much or too little emotion, both of which can interfere with learning. Often reflections focus too much on classroom management or building rapport with learners, and, while these are completely valid aspects of reflection, they may dominate the reflection to the detriment of academic, personal, social, and professional development, and transformational learning. Possibly, a lack of attention that educators place on addressing these shortfalls is the reason for a lack of criticality in service-learning reflections; yet this lack of critical reflection is something that needs to be addressed (Stewart, 2011). Wu and Dahlgren (2011), from their work with immigrant populations, note the seriousness of this, claiming that:

> the promise of service-learning may be overemphasized, as scholars all too often fail to report any challenges throughout service-learning programs or to comment on their critical reflections on such experiences. This is a significant flaw, as the essence of service-learning for preparing future educators must address the structured inequity that impacts people of color. A key part of this effort requires student teachers to *reflect critically* [my emphasis] on their stereotypes and biases in order to ensure service-learning programs that are based on mutual respect and the desire for social change. (pp. 264–265)

Because TESOL is a profession that works with learners who face frequent linguistic and social challenges, issues of social justice should be evident, yet they do not always arise in preservice teachers' reflections. There is a danger when these issues are not exposed in service-learning reflections, as Cho and Gulley (2017) point out: "without thoughtfully integrated TESOL education and reflection it [service-learning] can merely reinforce stereotypes of some student populations" (p. 630). Questions then arise: how can educators prompt critical reflection if preservice teachers do not understand the realities of diverse learners and their families or have a tendency to blame the victim? How can educators prompt critical reflections if preservice teachers hold a deficit view of teaching and see their role in service-learning as savior of the marginalized learners? Of course, as mentioned earlier, some forms of critical reflection may not be appropriate in some contexts, particularly those in which it may be risky to critique government policy or local traditions. In such cases, how can educators help preservice teachers reflect on ways to advocate for learners and encourage social change in a safe and effective way?

Another problem is that formats of reflection are often limited to traditional platforms, such as written journals and reflection papers, and group discussion (Stewart, 2011); yet the personal nature of reflection suggests that a single format may not be most conducive for learning for everyone and there is a need for varied, alternative approaches.

Although reflection is central to service-learning, it is challenging to assess and there are debates about how to do this (Gelmon et al., 2018; Molee et al., 2010). First of all, reflections rely on self-reported observations and data, which are very subjective and difficult to check. Then, as mentioned earlier, it may not be possible to assess dispositions or attitudes, given their personal and private nature, and questions arise about how to evaluate what someone thinks or feels about an experience, or even if it should be evaluated. Couple this with the fact that often reflections are assessed for "correctness" according to the expectations that educators set. In this way, educators hold the power in dictating what they think reflections should be, rather than being open to alternative understandings of what reflections can look like. Savvy students understand how to complete assignments according to their instructors' preferences, so they may write reflections that they feel instructors want, rather than reflections that are honest contemplations on observations or issues that arise in practice. This then makes learning less meaningful.

Finally, institutions do not necessarily encourage service-learning or reflective practice or have any kind of support structure to help make it part of the institutional culture (Jaeger, 2013). The focus of administration is typically on making sure that instructors have the basics to help their students produce good academic results. There is no time, or money, or opportunity to set up service-learning projects and a sustainable system of partners to mentor reflective practice. This can be a problem when it comes to preparing preservice ESOL teachers to make reflective practice "a way of life" (Farrell, 2019).

In summary, some of challenges and issues to be aware of regarding reflective practice in service-learning include:

- ensuring a shared understanding of what service-learning and reflective practice are
- reconciling expectations and guidance with personal reflection and creative thinking
- capitalizing on the benefits of frequent reflection while avoiding reflection fatigue
- effectively "teaching" or facilitating reflective practice
- fostering reflections that have focus, depth, and criticality

- helping to raise awareness of difficult issues, while avoiding prescriptive approaches to reflection and maintaining a safe, comfortable learning environment
- balancing academic requirements and grades for reflection with meaningful, honest, and personal learning
- finding institutional support for service-learning and developing a culture of reflection.

Given the challenges and issues associated with reflective practice in service-learning, it can be daunting to consider adding a service-learning approach into a TESOL course or program. The challenges and issues will be addressed in subsequent chapters.

> **Points for Reflection**
> - Considering the challenges in implementing service-learning and fostering effective reflections, do you believe it can be an effective pedagogical approach in TESOL? Why or why not?
> - Why do you think quality reflections with depth and focus and criticality are difficult for many ESOL preservice teachers?
> - How would you address the challenges presented above?
> - Is it necessary to assess reflections on service-learning in TESOL contexts?

CONCLUSION

Despite the challenges, the benefits of service-learning, including enhanced learning and the increase in community engagement and participants' sense of civic responsibility, have led to its use as a teaching and learning approach in various forms and contexts around the world. The overwhelmingly positive responses from community partners and preservice teachers in my own TESOL courses, as well as evidence of learning that I have observed through reflections and actions, convince me of the value of service-learning. Reflection, an essential part of service-learning, is explored more deeply in Chapter 2.

Chapter 2

Characterizing Reflective Practice in TESOL Service-Learning

INTRODUCTION

Despite the gender bias of the time, Huxley (1933), made a relevant point when he said, "Experience is not what happens to a man; it is what a man does with what happens to him" (p, 5). Similarly, the service-learning experience is not simply a requirement to meet in order to pass a course; it is an opportunity to learn and grow in multiple ways – academically, professionally, socially, and personally – as well as a way to contribute to the community, inform future practice, and lay groundwork for positive change. For any amount of learning – big or small – to happen, it is essential for participants to reflect meaningfully on the experience. Reflection is not simply about looking back. It is about reviewing experiences, yes, but also analyzing them in relation to existing knowledge, beliefs, experiences, and wider contexts. It is about making meaning from experiences, and using the new knowledge gained to make informed decisions about how to improve in future.

In this chapter we will look more closely at reflective practice in service-learning generally, and more specifically in a TESOL service-learning context. We will explore definitions and principles of reflective practice in education as they apply to service-learning contexts to help us unpack what reflective practice in TESOL service-learning looks like. Starting with Dewey's (1933) phases of reflective thought, we will discuss various models and frameworks, including Farrell's (2019) six principles of reflective practice in ELT. Because of its importance in service-learning pedagogy, additional emphasis is placed on critical reflection.

IMPORTANCE OF REFLECTIVE PRACTICE IN SERVICE-LEARNING

To start, think about your responses to the reflection questions below.

Points for Reflection
- How would you define "reflection" in an academic context?
- What is the purpose of reflection?
- What questions do you have about reflective practice?

The literature on reflective practice in TESOL service-learning is rather limited. That said, it is informed by important contributions made by advocates of service-learning experiences generally, starting with Dewey (1933, 1938), whose work on reflective experience and education is still relevant today. A little more recently, service-learning scholars (Ash et al., 2005; Eyler et al., 1996; Furco et al., 2010; Hatcher et al., 2004) have published important work on reflective practice. Eyler's (2002a) work on reflection in service-learning, though not specific to TESOL, stresses that "attaining the most important goals of service-learning is dependent on high quality programs that incorporate effective reflection" (p. 532). Farrell (2019) writes comprehensively about reflective practice in ELT, but not specifically in a service-learning context. While work in TESOL service-learning is increasing (Perren & Wurr, 2015; Wurr, 2018), a specific focus on reflective practice in this context is still limited. This chapter will attempt to fill the void, but first let's consider reflective practice in service-learning in general.

It is useful to reiterate the importance of reflective practice in service-learning – indeed, it is part of what defines service-learning. As noted in Chapter 1, service-learning is "a teaching and learning strategy that integrates meaningful community service with instruction and *reflection* [my emphasis] to enrich the learning experience, teach civic responsibility, and strengthen communities" (National Service-Learning Clearinghouse cited in Ryan, 2012, p. 4). Jacoby (2014) also stresses the importance of reflection in her interpretation of service-learning, "a form of experiential education in which students engage in activities that address human and community needs together with structured opportunities for *reflection* [my emphasis] designed to achieve desired learning outcomes" (p. 1). As such, reflection must do more than describe the service-learning experience; it must bring together the academic content and the service experience to demonstrate achievement of learning outcomes. Eyler (2002b) is often cited for her comment that "Reflection is the hyphen that links service to the learning" (p. 453). Similarly, Jacoby (2014) remarks that it is not service-learning without reflection because it is reflection that intentionally and purposely connects the " service" to the " learning" .

As educators, we may understand the importance of reflective practice in service-learning and how simply describing the service in a reflection is not enough, but what may still be unclear is what effective reflection looks like, how to facilitate it, and how to assess it. For some individuals, reflection in an academic context may be completely unfamiliar, as I learned in my own practice when a preservice ESOL teacher submitted a written reflection that described in detail (and considerable length) their feelings about a personal relationship, apartment chores, and troubling career plans. Likely, this individual was more familiar with reflections in the genre of a personal diary and presumably shared this personal information in order to explain their mental state during service-learning. As explained in Chapter 1, emotion is an important part of a reflection, but, by focusing on feelings without explicitly exploring them in connection with the experience and wider contexts, the reflection was not very meaningful. Reflecting on this myself, I realized that I had made the mistake of assuming that all preservice teachers knew what a written reflection in an academic context was. I had not made my expectations clear enough.

An important aspect of reflection is asking questions and, as I reflected on my expectations for students' reflections, multiple questions arose:

1. What is the purpose of reflection?
2. What exactly is reflection?
3. What is the process for reflection in service-learning?
4. What are the characteristics of reflection in service-learning?
5. What does reflection in service-learning look like?
6. What is the difference between reflection and critical reflection?
7. How is reflection in service-learning transformative?
8. How does reflective practice in TESOL service-learning compare with reflective practice in ELT?
9. (How) can reflective practice in service-learning be " taught" or facilitated?
10. How can reflections be assessed?

In the pages that follow, questions 1–8 will be addressed. Questions 9 and 10 will be addressed in Chapters 4 and 3 respectively.

WHAT IS THE PURPOSE OF REFLECTION?

The purpose of reflection is to enhance learning. Moon (2001) closely links the stages of learning to reflection, as shown by her five-stage framework for learning in higher education contexts:

1. *Noticing* refers to the identification of new information, material, or ideas.

2. *Making sense* means making ideas coherent, but without processing or connecting to other ideas.
3. *Making meaning* refers to the start of a deeper form of learning by integrating ideas, but with limited reach beyond the immediate context.
4. *Working with meaning* involves making connections to a broader context.
5. *Transformative learning* demonstrates a change in understandings as a result of a restructuring of ideas. (p. 6)

Moon (2001) suggests that, in the "making sense" stage of learning, we revisit information and ideas through reflection to find clarity. And when we "make meaning", connect to broader contexts, restructure ideas, and change our understandings, we engage in reflection. So, if we reflect as we process, reprocess, connect, and restructure information and ideas, it is not surprising that Moon further asserts that reflection improves cognitive ability, encourages metacognition (awareness of one's own thinking), and enables ownership of learning.

Rogers (2002) also highlights the importance of making meaning, strongly asserting that "[t]he creation of meaning out of experience is at the very heart of what it means to be human. It enables us to make sense of and attribute value to the events of our lives" (p. 848). In the context of service-learning, these notions of learning through reflection are echoed. Vanderbilt University's Office of Active Citizenship and Learning (n.d.), goes so far as to claim that "'Reflection' is just another word for learning. What distinguishes it from other forms of learning is that 'reflection' grows out of experience" ("Importance of Reflection in service-learning"). In TESOL service-learning, meaning or understanding can come when connections are made between experiences in community and theories of language learning pedagogy and/ or ideas discussed in classes and readings. Preservice ESOL teachers are expected to work towards meeting academic outcomes and develop their ELT knowledge and skills and beliefs while working with community partners to meet needs, improve understanding and future practice, and ideally, contribute to social justice goals. As mentioned earlier, reflection is not simply about looking back. The purpose is to engage multiple cognitive processes to build understanding, to learn, improve, and apply the learning to future actions. In service-learning, therefore, the goal of reflection is to help participants develop academically, cognitively, professionally, socially, civically, and personally.

Points for Reflection
- Do you agree that "creating meaning out of experience is at the very heart of what it means to be human" (Roger, 2002, p. 848)?
- To what extent do you agree that "reflection" is another word for learning? (Vanderbilt University's Office of Active Citizenship and Learning, n.d.)

WHAT EXACTLY IS REFLECTION?

John Dewey (1910, 1933) emphasizes the importance of experience for education, specifying that, for learning to take place, it must involve reflective thinking. He defines reflective thought as "Active, persistent, and careful consideration of any belief or supposed form of knowledge in the light of the grounds that support it, and the further conclusions to which it tends" (1933, p. 9). In other words, he views reflection as more complex than simply contemplating or pondering something. Rather, it is a systematic inquiry or process involving a suspension of judgement until adequate evidence is intentionally collected and analyzed to support responses that affect further experiences. Before exploring the process, let's consider other definitions of reflective practice.

Hatton and Smith (1995) synthesize various research studies on reflection in teacher education and define it simply as "deliberate thinking about action with a view to its improvement" (p. 40). This is not to say that reflection or reflective practice is a term that is easily defined. Farrell (2019) writes comprehensively about multiple interpretations and approaches to reflective practice in ELT, acknowledging the need to share some understanding of what reflective practice is, but also to make informed decisions about defining it in specific contexts. He defines reflective practice in ELT as:

> a cognitive process accompanied by a set of attitudes in which teachers systematically collect data about their practice, and, while engaging in dialogue with others, use the data to make informed decisions about their practice both inside and outside the classroom. (p. 28)

Farrell arrived at this definition by building on Dewey (1910, 1933) and others (Brookfield, 1995; Hatton & Smith, 1995; Kolb, 1984; Schön, 1983, 1987; to name a few).

In service-learning, similar themes appear in definitions of reflective practice. For example, the notion of a systematic process and words like *deliberate* and *intentional* are common. Making connections between the service experience and learning is crucial, as conveyed by terms such as *cognition, academic development, informed, growth* and *progress*. To illustrate, Hatcher and Bringle (1997), whose service-learning work is seminal, define reflection as "the intentional consideration of an experience in light of particular learning objectives" (p. 153). Often in service-learning, connections between the intellectual and the emotional in terms of self-awareness and attitude are stressed (Rogers, 2002; Stewart, 2011), which echoes Farrell (2019) and Dewey (1933). Stewart's (2011) definition of reflection in service-learning is:

a deliberate practice of thinking about past experiences or knowledge in order to make meaning, enable better choices or actions, or increase effectiveness in future attempts. In other words, reflection is a constructivist act that serves to transform a learners' schema. (pp. 38–39)

Reference to improving future practice, transformative learning, and building a better world are commonly associated with reflection in both ELT and in service-learning. This again builds on Dewey's work, which stresses the need to question values and beliefs, consider alternative views, and challenge existing norms and simplistic solutions (Jacoby, 2014). These processes add a critical perspective to the concept of reflective practice, which is encouraged in service-learning contexts.

Points for Reflection

- Do any of these definitions cause you to rethink your own definition of reflection?
- In your view, is reflection in service-learning different from reflection on traditional academic experiences?
- In what ways do you think that reflective practice can:
  - be systematic and intentional?
  - connect the intellectual and emotional?
  - connect experience and learning?
  - involve questioning of values and beliefs?
  - challenge existing norms and simplistic solutions and consider alternative views?
  - transform learning?
  - work towards building a better world?

WHAT IS THE PROCESS FOR REFLECTION IN SERVICE-LEARNING?

Dewey's (1933) reflective process comprises six phases: experience – suggesting – intellectualizing – hypothesizing – reasoning – testing the hypothesis. To illustrate these phases, consider a TESOL service-learning context where a preservice ESOL teacher observes that an EL is not responding to questions. This is the experience phase. Initially, the preservice teacher may interpret this as a language deficiency (suggesting phase). Later, in thinking more about the experience, the preservice teacher realizes that there might be other reasons for the learner's lack of response and so decides to explore further (intellectualizing phase). In talking with peers and teachers, other possible explanations are suggested, like boredom, lack of confidence, shyness, poorly crafted questions, unfamiliarity with expectations, lack of content knowledge, fatigue or health issues, and so on (hypothesizing phase). The preservice teacher collects more data through questioning and comparisons with other samples of the learner's work, finding that neither language, nor content, nor confidence, shyness, or health were the problem. Revisiting the question prompts reveals that the way they were worded may have lacked clarity and specifics (reasoning phase). The preservice teacher then restructures the questions, provides additional scaffolding, conducts further observation, and resolves to work harder on developing questioning skills (testing the hypothesis phase). Why this problem emerged raises additional questions and issues. It is possible that the preservice teacher had not spent enough time planning the types of questions and monitoring comprehension, or they had overconfidence in their ability to develop and ask questions, or about the learner's ability to unpack questions and respond. To address these and other questions throughout the service-learning experience, it is necessary for preservice teachers to question their beliefs, and preconceived ideas about their own identity and about how they (and others) interact with ELs and diverse populations. Questions about the broader environment can also be asked, like has the EL been made to feel welcome in the community? By exploring further questions, the reflection process continues. An important point for Dewey (1933) and critical service-learning advocates is that reflection must consider the impact of the experience, challenge beliefs and assumptions, and consider future action. It is this aspect of reflection that has the greatest potential to transform learning.

The process for reflection thus includes intentional and systematic data gathering to highlight examples of learning or lack thereof by the preservice teacher and/or the EL or community participants. It also involves asking a lot of questions to explore multiple facets of an experience. This is made easier by interacting with others in pre, during, or post-experience meetings with peers, instructors, and community partners. Exploring experiences and questions with others is important for exchanging perspectives and insights and developing understanding for future action.

WHAT ARE THE CHARACTERISTICS OF REFLECTION IN SERVICE-LEARNING?

The characteristics of effective reflections are typically based on various standards, indicators, principles, and models of reflection, a few of which are presented here.

To emphasize the importance of reflection in service-learning, the United States National Youth Leadership Council (NYLC) (2008) includes a standard for reflection within their list of research-based service-learning standards. It states that "[s]ervice-learning incorporates multiple challenging reflection activities that are ongoing and that prompt deep thinking and analysis about oneself and one's relationship to society" ("Reflection" section). There are five indicators listed for this standard:

1.   Service-learning reflection includes a variety of verbal, written, artistic, and nonverbal activities to demonstrate understanding and changes in participants' knowledge, skills, and/or attitudes.
2.   Service-learning reflection occurs before, during, and after the service experience.
3.   Service-learning reflection prompts participants to think deeply about complex community problems and alternative solutions.
4.   Service-learning reflection encourages participants to examine their preconceptions and assumptions in order to explore and understand their roles and responsibilities as citizens.
5.   Service-learning reflection encourages participants to examine a variety of social and civic issues related to their service-learning experience so that participants understand connections to public policy and civic life.

To some extent these indicators are interconnected and may seem to overlap, for example, thinking deeply about community problems (indicator 3) may be focused on problems in the local experience but it could also lead participants to consider social injustices or problematic policies in the broader community (indicator 5). While both relate to civic responsibility, indicator 5 takes a more explicit critical lens. Although these indicators were created specifically for elementary and secondary schools, they could easily apply to other contexts as well.

Points for Reflection
- How realistic is it to expect that knowledge, skills, and attitudes can change through reflection on service-learning experience (NYLC indicator 1)?
- Would your students be able to identify complex community problems and think deeply about alternative solutions (NYLC indicator 3)? If not, what kind of guidance might be needed?
- Would your students have any difficulty identifying and examining preconceptions and assumptions and exploring their role as responsible citizens (indicator 4)? If so, what could help them achieve this goal?
- How might "examining a variety of social and civic issues related to their service-learning experience so that participants understand connections to public policy and civic life" (indicator 5) be relevant to TESOL service-learning?

Parallels exist between these NYLC indicators for reflection and the principles of reflection in service-learning devised by Eyler et al. (1996). They found that the most effective reflections are characterized by four Cs: *continuous, connected, challenging,* and *contextualized.*

The "first c", *continuous,* means that reflection should be done before, during, and after service. It also means in a cyclical manner, with feedback, which equates to NYLC indicator 2.

The "second c", *connected,* refers to connections in two aspects. One is linking academic learning with the service experience. Reflective practice in service-learning specifically requires the integration of reflection on service with the reflection on academics so that target academic outcomes can be met through the service (Hatcher & Bringle, 1997). This type of connection aligns to NYLC indicator 1, whereby existing knowledge, skills, and attitudes learned in the classroom are linked to the practical experience part of service-learning. The second aspect of connection is linking the service experience to broader concepts and social issues. This type of connection aligns with NYLC indicators 3 and 5, in which participants connect observations they make during the practical experience to community problems and broader social issues.

Challenge, Eyler et al.'s (1996) "third c", purports that reflections should *challenge* assumptions and beliefs, compelling participants to think more critically about their own beliefs and values. This principle is closely related to NYLC indicators 4 and 5, whereby an individual's assumptions and beliefs are challenged through self-analysis and institutionalized norms and assumptions are challenged through more critical reflection. It is this aspect that often pushes students out of their comfort zones.

Context, the "fourth c" means that reflections should be purposeful and meaningful for the *context.* This principle relates to levels of formality and authenticity of the various reflection activities. For example, the earlier example of the preservice ESOL teacher writing a descriptive, emotional, diary-style reflection did not match the academic context. At the same time, if a reflection is too academic, it can become a contrived exercise rather than a meaningful learning tool. Context is not explicitly stated in the NYLC indicators, which are only broad guidelines, so instructors need to plan reflection activities with context in mind and provide tools to facilitate reflective practice (see Chapter 4 for more on facilitating reflective practice).

The four Cs inform models or frameworks that are used to facilitate effective reflections. In their service-learning reflection framework, DEAL, Ash et al. (2005, p. 51) emphasize learning. DEAL consists of three stages: (1) describing, (2) examining, (3) articulating learning (AL). In the AL stage of reflection, students demonstrate their learning from the service-learning experience in three growth areas: academic, civic, and personal. Four prompt questions are used to guide the AL stage of reflection:

1. What did I learn?

2.   How, specifically, did I learn it?
3.   Why does this learning matter, or why is it significant?
4.   In what ways will I use this learning, or what goals shall I set in accordance with what I have learned in order to improve myself, the quality of my learning, or the quality of my future experiences or service?

Reflections are written responses to these questions using a cyclical approach with iterations of reflections and feedback repeated throughout the semester. As such, reflections can be characterized by responses addressing the questions: what, how, why, and what now.

While characteristics of reflections in service-learning can be drawn from standards, indicators, principles, and models, it is useful to remember that they are not prescribed. Reflections in service-learning should represent meaningful thinking, unique to individuals and the context.

WHAT DOES REFLECTION IN SERVICE-LEARNING LOOK LIKE?

We can't see thoughts or reflection as they occur in the mind, so we rely on verbal, written or other representations (graphic, artistic) of reflections to make thinking visible. With the reflection process and characteristics in mind, let's think more specifically about what reflections in service-learning might look like. It helps to draw on the definitions and essential elements of service-learning cited in Chapter 1 to identify key aspects that might be included in service-learning reflections, such as *achieving learning outcomes*, *identifying meaningful experiences*, *developing civic responsibility*, and *strengthening community*. "Meaningful experiences" might be displayed through comments that reveal an ability to identify events or interactions that lead to demonstrated English learning, or disengagement, or relevant issues, as well as events or interactions that elicit a need for exploration into impacts and causes. In terms of "developing civic responsibility" and "strengthening community", comments might reflect self-identity, importance of collaboration with community partners, and importantly, suggestions for future improvement and engagement.

Ash et al. (2005) look for evidence of three target areas of growth or development displayed in service-learning reflections, namely academic, civic, and personal. Grouping areas of development into categories can help organize target growth areas and enable instructors (and students) to more easily track progress. They can also help frame expectations in reflections. When I think about the areas of growth that I want my TESOL students to demonstrate in their service-learning reflections, I expand Ash et al.'s three areas to the following four categories:

- Academic/cognitive development
- Professional development
- Social development/civic engagement
- Personal growth.

The categories are very broad, and Table 2.1 illustrates how I have narrowed them down into specific knowledge, skills, competencies, and dispositions that might be described in TESOL reflections. The lists for each category are not prescriptive, nor are they exhaustive. In addition, it is acknowledged that there are overlaps between categories and this is indicated by the circle connecting the categories at the center.

Points for Reflection
- To what extent do you agree that the four development categories that I use in my TESOL service-learning context (Table 2.1) are important aspects to reflect on?
- Which areas of development do you think students in your context need to reflect on? How would you modify the categories to apply to your context? What knowledge, skills, and dispositions would you add to the lists?

Table 2.1. Sample categories of development in service-learning

Academic/cognitive development	Professional development
Link theory and practice	Develop ELT competencies
Apply knowledge (language teaching and learning theory) to new contexts	Show success in taking on increased responsibility
Develop critical thinking	Develop understanding of professional opportunities
Develop observation and perception skills	Gain confidence in career choice
Develop metacognition	
Build high order thinking skills-analysis, evaluation, problem-solving	
Develop critical reflection skills	

Social/civic development	Personal growth
Develop empathy	Build self-confidence
Increase interpersonal skills, including communication skills	Develop sense of personal identity and its effects
Increase awareness of and support for diverse learners	Develop self-awareness
Show openness to others' perspectives & ideas	Show openness to change (ideas, values, beliefs)
Build teamwork skills	Develop curiosity and disposition of inquiry
Develop leadership skills	View service-learning as positive experience
Develop sense of civic responsibility	

Each of the four categories of development is discussed below in relation to how they might be demonstrated in TESOL service-learning reflections.

Academic/Cognitive Development

Academic development refers to the course knowledge and skills that students are expected to develop during the service-learning experience. Typically, this refers to the ability to link theory and practice, and apply knowledge in new contexts. Reflections displaying this might involve evaluating incidents in the community using knowledge previously learned, or examining reasons for incidents or interactions based on theoretical concepts learned in the course. To illustrate what reflections might look like, it is useful to see examples. In my undergraduate TESOL course at a US university, during a service-learning project at a local elementary school, one preservice teacher observed that an Arabic-speaking learner often omitted the auxiliary verb, "do", as in *I not like reading*, and they reflected that this could be a result of first language transference because in Arabic there is no equivalent for "do" (Smith, 2001). This provided evidence that they were linking theory and practice.

Eyler (2002a) points out that "reflection is the mechanism for stimulating cognitive development" (p. 522). Indeed, cognitive development involves growth in critical reflection skills, critical thinking, problem-solving, metacognition, and other high order thinking skills that are valued in academic contexts. But this can be challenging. For example, problem-solving in service-learning can be difficult because the problems "are not easy to identify and define and there are no clear answers about how to resolve them" (Eyler, 2002a, p. 521). For this reason, support and reassurance for participants in service-learning is important. Metacognition is valued in service-learning reflections because being aware of one's own thinking helps determine what and how to improve. This can lead to changes in one's thinking, which illustrates transformative learning.

Points for Reflection

- Consider the following reflection, written by a preservice teacher in my TESOL course at the end of a service-learning project in a local school: "In the beginning, I thought that I knew what was best for the ELs. However, I was wrong. I learned not to underestimate their abilities and I learned that I need to get more information before making decisions about what is best."

- To what extent do you think the reflection above represents cognitive development?

Professional Development

Professional development may at times overlap with academic/cognitive development but generally focuses on specific competencies, skills, and attitudes related to a particular career rather than general subject knowledge or cognitive skills. Professional competencies in TESOL would include using techniques to scaffold language learning, or using strategies to deal with language errors (for more examples see Table 4.3 , p. 94). Demonstrations of professional growth can be captured in reflections that connect TESOL course instruction and events or interactions experienced in service-learning. For example, during an oral debriefing, one preservice teacher in my TESOL course, commented that she was unsure about how to differentiate instruction until she actually faced it during the service-learning project and realized that she could skillfully apply it. Specifically, she explained that, rather than what she thought would be a chaotic classroom with 20 different activities and ELs competing for the teacher's attention, she was able to assign several different but related activities in which some learners worked alone to write paragraphs while others, writing on the same topic, used sentence frames as scaffolding, or worked with partners using a peer-teaching approach; and this freed her to work with another group of ELs who needed more direct support with their writing. Her reflection revealed that she had moved beyond her academic knowledge of the concept to actually developing her professional competence in an authentic setting.

Other aspects of professional development might include developing understanding of career opportunities, and gaining confidence in career choice. Service-learning is very useful for this last point because it gives preservice teachers direct experience working with ELs in an authentic setting, hence a little insight into what their future career might be like. In reflecting on the experience in a service-learning project at a local elementary school, one preservice teacher in my TESOL course commented that working with the younger learners made her want to change her studies from secondary education to elementary education. In another example, a preservice teacher came to the realization that he was not interested in teaching after all. Of course, this would not be a desired outcome, but if he was not truly committed to teaching, it was better for everyone that he come to this conclusion early.

Points for Reflection
- What specific TESOL competencies would you expect preservice ESOL teachers to reflect on during a service-learning experience?
- How important is it in your TESOL context for preservice teachers to reflect on their career choice?

Social/Civic Development

Social development involves observing and interacting with others. From this, preservice teachers working with community members might develop their sense of empathy, interpersonal and communication skills, cultural awareness, openness to others' perspectives and ideas, sense of civic responsibility, to name a few examples. Empathy is particularly important in TESOL as we need to help teachers work effectively with diverse members of the community. Often these populations are marginalized and sometimes service-learning participants view them as helpless and needing "saving", rather than as capable individuals who are contributing members of the community from whom we all might learn something. How one interacts with people and communities is important in service-learning as it can help develop a sense of civic responsibility and community mindedness – other indicators of social development.

Reflections on social development can be supported with descriptions of specific interactions. For example, one preservice teacher in my TESOL course reflected on her communication skills when thinking about how she struggled to get ELs to follow instructions during the service-learning project. In the end she realized that she had been speaking too quickly and needed to slow down and break instructions down into more manageable chunks for some learners. Reflections might also refer to what preservice teachers learned about an EL's culture or language or past educational experience. Reflections on civic development might refer to how a participant might continue to engage in community development or advocate for multicultural populations in the future.

Points for Reflection
- What aspects of social development would you try to foster in a TESOL service-learning context?
- What do you think reflections about civic responsibility or effective citizenship might look like in your context?

Some qualities in the area of social/civic development, such as empathy and sense of civic identity overlap with personal growth. Instructors need to decide how to form and define categories that best meet their needs. For purposes of distinction, I have categorized aspects that directly involve other people as part of social development, and those that don't directly involve other people as part of personal growth.

Personal Growth

Areas of personal growth involve the development of self-awareness and individual qualities or character-building traits, like self-confidence, adaptability, a sense of curiosity and disposition of inquiry. Importantly, self-awareness involves having a sense of personal identity and an openness to change in terms of beliefs, ideas, or values. Reflecting on personal growth, more than the other areas of development, requires that we put ourselves into a vulnerable position, where we can self-analyze and self-critique, which can be uncomfortable for some people. For this reason, support and reassurance should be available, and participants should not be forced to share personal reflections that they don't want to.

Points for Reflection

- Consider this excerpt from the reflection journal of a preservice teacher in my TESOL course during a service-learning project at a local school:

  > When teaching my lesson, there were things that did not go according to plan. While the whole plan was not derailed, there were instances where I had to think on my feet to adapt to the needs of the learners in the moment. This is something I do not have as much experience with, but definitely feel more confident doing after having the experience to teach my lesson in front of real-life English learners.

- In your view, how might this reflection illustrate personal growth or development?

In the reflection excerpt above, the preservice teacher acknowledges weaknesses (*did not go according to plan*) and a lack of experience. This demonstrates a willingness to expose their vulnerabilities. Recognizing personal adaptability and growing confidence demonstrates self-awareness.

Most proponents of service-learning would agree that the aspects of *achieving learning outcomes, identifying meaningful experiences, developing civic responsibility*, and *strengthening community* should be evident in reflections at some point. Reflections should also display evidence of development and growth. In some contexts, a social justice approach may also be encouraged. Of course, reflection is a continuous process and not everything will be included in every reflection. In addition, some learning may be displayed implicitly rather than explicitly.

Points for Reflection

- Consider the following reflection from the journal of an undergraduate pre-service teacher in my TESOL course. The service-learning project involved participating in an after-school ESL program for young learners at a local low-income school. Here, they were observing their classmates teach. Note that this was just an excerpt from an ongoing reflection journal.

  > During the vocab presentation lesson, my classmate did an excellent job integrating the language and content. Rather than just asking them questions on definitions, she made the effort to contextualize the vocabulary words with the story. It seemed that her intent with these visuals was to have students notice how all of the words interact together in the context of the theme and most students were engaged. I wonder if some of them, however, were lost because ELs seemed to be a bit distracted. Maybe 14 vocabulary words at a time is too much for these students. I would possibly suggest breaking it down into more manageable chunks. She asked great metacognitive and noticing questions during this activity. She gave students appropriate wait-time to answer her questions (SIOP strategy) and she picked a variety of students rather than just letting the same student answer the question.

- What key aspects of service-learning (achieving learning outcomes, identifying meaningful experiences, developing civic responsibility, strengthening community) or target developmental areas (academic/cognitive, professional, social/civic, personal) does the reflection journal excerpt display?
- What might you like to know more about? What questions could you ask this preservice teacher to foster deeper reflection?

In analyzing the reflection journal excerpt above, we see that the writer describes the observation of a vocabulary presentation that the classmate taught. They evaluate the teaching by commenting on positive aspects of the teaching and identifying areas that might be done differently, which displays cognitive development (evaluation). They make explicit links to academic theory by citing the SIOP (Sheltered Instruction Observation Protocol) model that was discussed in the TESOL methods course, demonstrating some evidence of *achieving learning outcomes*; hence, academic development. This reflection could be considered an example of a *meaningful experience* because it identifies an issue, considers the cause and impact (some ELs are lost), and makes a suggestion for improving future practice (reduce the number of vocabulary words). This reflection does not touch on *civic responsibility* or *strengthening community*. It is expected that other aspects and other areas of development might be evident in other reflections.

In summary, reflections that identify and explain growth in the areas of academic/cognitive, professional, social/civic, and personal development (or similar categories) are typically expected in service-learning. Regular opportunities are provided for reflection, so not all of these aspects would be evident in every reflection. While development in the target areas clearly benefits the individual, it also benefits the community in the long term because these skills and dispositions also contribute to the development of more community-minded and responsible citizens, which ultimately strengthens the community as a whole. More can be said about *strengthening community*, so we turn to that next.

STRENGTHENING COMMUNITIES

Strengthening the community is somewhat broad and needs attention. Community could refer to the learning community whereby reflections commonly show evidence of how participants learn from each other. In most cases, however, community in service-learning refers to building collaborative and sustainable partnerships between universities and schools and local organizations where everyone contributes and everyone benefits as they work together and learn from each other in pursuit of the goals.

Opportunities should be provided for reflections on how the service-learning experience helped address an identified community need. The identified needs are highly contextualized to the specific community and reflections should be relevant to that context. Within the TESOL service-learning context, the development of professional skills can ultimately help strengthen communities because developing effective ESOL teachers who advocate for ELs will have positive impacts on the community. In their reflections, preservice teachers might comment on how their English teaching skills are developing, or they may reflect on observations of how the ELs may be benefiting.

Points for Reflection

- Consider the reflection below in terms of how it might display a strengthening of the community. It was written by a preservice teacher in my TESOL course, who reflects on the experience of reading a story about a pet iguana to the ELs during our service-learning project at an elementary school:

  On reflection, I realized that I did not say everything I wanted to or that I had planned to, and I should have had students do more

> interacting. This is such an easy thing to do – "Turn and talk to your neighbor, do you think Alex will get the pet iguana?" It would have given students a little bit of time to process and practice articulating opinions before they had to share in front of the whole group. Although I am disappointed I didn't include any of this, I think this experience will ensure that I always include peer interaction in my future lessons.

- What is your impression of the reflection excerpt above?

While evidence of strengthening the community is not directly evident in the reflection above, the excerpt does demonstrate that this preservice teacher learned something from the experience. The preservice teacher realized that the teacher-centered approach may have been detrimental to learning and suggests that peer interaction would have been easy and beneficial for learning, and explains why. By committing to improving practice in the future, this participant shows progress on the way to becoming a more effective teacher, who is self-aware and committed to improving their teaching. It is hoped that the community where this preservice teacher eventually teaches will benefit from having a reflective teacher.

Ideally, there also should be opportunities for the community partner to reflect so that all voices can be included. In such cases, post-service reflections could include contributions from community partners in online platforms. The development of relationships between students and community groups that might not otherwise meet are made possible by service-learning and go some way towards strengthening the community. It should be noted that research on service-learning reflections from the community perspective is not prevalent in the literature and there needs to be more work in this area (Tauscher Birdsall, n.d.).

Finally, from a more critical lens, the community can be strengthened by identifying and challenging injustices. To this end, preservice teachers might question norms, and reflect on why ELs need advocates, and they might explore ways to work towards addressing injustices. This can be difficult, but the first-hand experience that service-learning provides allows participants to observe and interact with ELs in a way they cannot through their regular coursework, and through reflecting on the experience, they may gain insights into the challenges and injustices that ELs face.

What reflections look like will depend on the individual, the context, and purpose of the reflection, but instructors should expect that essential aspects of service-learning and target development areas would be demonstrated in reflections at certain points.

WHAT IS THE DIFFERENCE BETWEEN REFLECTION AND CRITICAL REFLECTION?

Interpretations of reflection in service-learning vary by context, as they do in teacher education. In ELT, Farrell (2019) presents a clear explanation of what he refers to as weak and strong forms of reflection. The weak form refers to evaluation of one's practice in a limited way, often relying on a "gut feeling" or memory of what happened in a lesson. This form of reflection does not usually result in improvements, and may in fact be harmful, as teachers may second-guess what they actually did. In contrast, the strong form refers to systematically collecting and analyzing evidence and using it to make informed decisions about improving practice. The strong form of reflection typically involves an exploration of the causes and impacts of actions. Because this strong form often involves a consideration of multiple perspectives, and the questioning of beliefs, it is known as critical reflection.

Another form of critical reflection is concerned with equity issues and social justice education. This type of critical reflection goes beyond the current experience to question and discuss concerns about broader social and political issues related to culture and language and education in order to promote diversity and inclusion and advance equity so that future change can occur (Gorski & Dalton; Hill-Jackson & Lewis, 2011; Jacoby, 2014). This is relevant to TESOL service-learning where diverse populations are the focus. Language educators can help expose, explore, and demystify common misconceptions, untruths, and stereotypes that lead to structural inequality and discrimination based on social differences (Nieto, 2018), and, if it is appropriate for the context, promote agency for social change. If the purpose of education, as Dewey (1916) advocates, is to improve humanity by preparing students to be responsible members of democratic society, then there is much work to do. I do not mean that instructors should tell participants what to think, or what to reflect on, or prescribe a particular type of reflection; rather instructors can encourage reflection that connects education and experience in a way that raises awareness of issues and a consideration of ways to make positive change. Some might argue that not raising such awareness would be a disservice.

For Brookfield (1995) reflecting deeply on experience in an educational context is not reflecting critically. He explains that reflection becomes critical in two ways:

> The first is to understand how considerations of power undergird, frame, and distort educational processes and interactions. The second is to question assumptions and practices that seem to make our teaching lives easier but actually work against our own best long-term interests. (p. 8)

This means thinking past personal understandings and feelings to more complex processes, like challenging accepted norms, asking difficult questions, identifying social problems and injustices, and seeking change. This can be unsettling for some individuals, but it is through this kind of critical reflection that transformative learning can occur.

In a service-learning context, Jacoby (2014) expands on Brookfield's two ways of being critical. She identifies four meanings and applications of the word critical as it applies to service-learning. For one, reflection is a *critical* or *vital* part of service-learning. A second meaning views critical reflection as helping to develop *critical thinking* – a central goal of education generally, which compels us to look beyond first appearances and consider multiple perspectives. The third meaning of critical refers to *critical* or *essential questions* about "why things are and the attempt to fully understand the root causes of observable events and behaviors" (Eyler et al., 1996, p. 14), as well as questions about our beliefs, values, and assumptions. A final meaning for *critical* refers to a *critique* of society, distribution of power, and the important work in pursuing social justice. Jacoby (2014) defines critical reflection as "the process of analyzing, reconsidering, and questioning one's experiences within a broad context of issues and content knowledge" (p. 27). The "broad context of issues" that might be encountered in service-learning involve social injustices, like cultural and linguistic discrimination, racism, and stereotyping. Jacoby echoes Dewey when she points out that experience without critical reflection can be superficial, and "too easily allow students to reinforce their stereotypes about people who are different from themselves, develop simplistic solutions to complex problems, and generalize inaccurately based on limited data" (p. 27). To understand what Jacoby means by this, consider participants, who, after working with refugees in a service-learning context, claim to know what it is like to be a refugee or how to help them. To avoid eliciting reflections that include such simplistic statements and generalizations, instructors can facilitate critical reflection, where complex issues are explored, assumptions are challenged, and hard questions are asked. Jacoby (2014) asserts that:

> One can do service and one can learn, but reflection is the process through which the service and learning can become transformative. It is through critical reflection that we open ourselves to become changed in meaningful ways by what we do, whom we meet, what we know, and what we seek to know. (p. 50)

In other words, by critically reflecting on service-learning experiences, participants can transform themselves and work towards creating a more just world.

Van Leeuwen et al. (2017) also claim that critical reflection in community service-learning (CSL) is important when they assert:

> Discomfort serves as an important pedagogy in CSL since it asks students to radically reevaluate their worldview, playing a significant role in teaching and learning about "difficult" issues such as racism, oppression, and social injustice ... Through critical reflection, students can learn about themselves, develop a greater understanding of their personal strengths and limitations, and become better able to recognize and understand the political, economic, and social conditions that impact the community. (p. 131)

For example, before experiencing service-learning at a local food bank, participants may not have thought about why there is hunger in their town. Before experiencing a service-learning project at a local community center, participants may not have considered why some people need this community support. Discussing sensitive topics like hunger and poverty can be difficult, but some instructors may feel that if they remain silent or avoid such topics they risk perpetuating misunderstandings or sending the message that such problems are normalized.

In a multicultural service-learning context, Hill-Jackson and Lewis (2011) are more forceful in their assertion that:

> knowledge, skills, and social justice dispositions are mandatory features of a teacher candidate's preparatory experience [so] multicultural service-learning experiences [must] include the necessary theoretical and pedagogical framework, but also include a social justice dimension that demands critical introspection and reflection. (p. 313)

Similarly, Gorski and Dalton (2020), working in multicultural and social justice teacher education strongly agree and claim that:

> [b]y focusing on goals such as assimilation and celebrating diversity without attending to more critical goals, these approaches can cultivate in educators a false sense of preparedness to advocate for equity while obscuring the realities of racism, economic injustice, and other forms of oppression ... If learners can strengthen their abilities to do so [reflect critically], not just in retrospect but also in day-to-day practice – while interacting with economically marginalized children, for example – they are better prepared to adjust their ideologies or worldviews toward a social justice stance. (p. 359)

Consider the example of the refugee resettlement organization CSL. Reading about refugees in class is different from working with them directly, or with an organization where students can see the challenges and the available services and resources (or lack thereof). Service-learning can increase awareness of social issues because it engages students outside of familiar educational settings and compels them to observe how other people may be affected by particular issues. Critical reflection here might involve exploring why refugees struggle or are oppressed. Discussions can include ways to raise awareness of the challenges that refugees face or how they are treated in society. The goal of critical reflection in this sense is to help preservice teachers build greater understanding and challenge their beliefs and values, improve practice, and advocate for social justice in the communities in which they work. Suggestions on ways to facilitate critical reflection are presented in Chapter 4.

My intention in presenting these various interpretations of critical reflection is to raise awareness of different views, not to prescribe one over another. It is up to instructors to determine the form of reflection that best meets the needs of the service-learning experience in their context.

Points for Reflection
- What are the social issues in your context that students should be aware of?
- What kind of service-learning projects could help raise this awareness?
- Can you think of a context in which it may not be appropriate to encourage students to reflect critically?

HOW IS REFLECTION IN SERVICE-LEARNING TRANSFORMATIVE?

Hullender et al. (2015) borrow Mezirow's 2000 definition of transformative learning, which is "the process by which we transform our taken-for-granted frames of reference, e.g., perspectives, habits of mind, mind-sets, to make them more inclusive, discriminating, open, emotionally capable of change, and reflective so that they may generate beliefs and opinions that will prove more true or justified to guide action" (p. 59). Transformative learning, as such, is a result of critical reflection whereby we question our perspectives and beliefs, challenge our assumptions and restructure or change our thinking. Kiely (2005) asserts that "the ideal end result of transformational learning is that one is empowered by learning to be more socially responsible, self-directed, and less dependent on false assumptions" (p. 7), but he adds that this goal is not always achieved in service-learning. He argues, however, that there are multiple processes and levels of transformation and what he calls "nonreflective learning", which should also be valued as it can lead to long-term transformation. He thus expands on Mezirow's (2000) concept of transformation by suggesting a transformative learning model for service-learning. (For more on Kiely's work, see Chapter 3.)

Reflection on service-learning experiences may be considered transformative when, in the process of reflection, participants are compelled to think in a different way or adopt perspectives that they had not considered before. This requires honest self-examination and self-analysis in terms of how participants interacted or engaged with events and people at the community site. For a simple example, in a service-learning context, a preservice teacher in my TESOL course explained how their disbelief transformed to belief when they reflected on an observation during service-learning:

> The two boys I was working with were great at self-monitoring/noticing. I would ask the students to read the sentence they had just written, and I saw them correcting their errors as they read. It was very interesting to witness in person, as we have done lots of studying on these ideas but I didn't actually believe it would happen.

Transformation might also include finding a solution to a problem faced during the experience that was previously thought to be unsolvable, or realizing that a particular career path was wrong for an individual, or discovering that community engagement is something that an individual decides to continue beyond the end of the academic course.

For a more critical transformation, reflecting on their performance during service-learning requires participants to question and challenge the accepted norms that have shaped their beliefs making them think or act the way they do. For example, a participant in service-learning at a refugee resettlement organization, who may have previously been unaware of an asset-based view of refugees, might later decide that they want to continue working for the organization and help highlight the strengths of the refugees for potential employers, or perhaps start a public campaign to raise awareness of the contributions that refugees make in the community. Such examples of transformation in service-learning would meet the goals of transformative learning expressed by Hullender et al. (2015), Mezirow (2000), and Kiely (2005).

Points for Reflection
- Do you think learning can take place without transformation of some kind?

HOW DOES REFLECTIVE PRACTICE IN TESOL SERVICE-LEARNING COMPARE WITH REFLECTIVE PRACTICE IN ELT?

I agree with Farrell (2019) who is careful to point out that instructors should define reflective practice in a way that meets needs in their context. At the same time, he recognizes that understandings should be informed by accepted models of reflective practice, so that there is some fidelity to the process. Based on his study of existing models, he developed his own set of six interacting principles to inform reflective practice in ELT:

1. Reflective practice is holistic
2. Reflective practice is evidence-based
3. Reflective practice involves dialogue
4. Reflective practice bridges principles and practices
5. Reflective practice requires an inquiring disposition
6. Reflective practice is a way of life

Farrell's principles equally apply to reflective practice in TESOL service-learning. For example, reflective practice in service-learning is holistic in that it involves cognitive, metacognitive, *and* affective reflection on academic, professional, social, and personal growth, including development of civic responsibility and community. To emphasize affect, Stewart (2011) explains that reflection in service-learning must be multilayered, contemplative, and spiritual. He argues that it is naïve to think that participants can detach from their spiritual selves. In essence, he advocates for contemplative practices through introspection, which he explains as "the ability of a learner to self-observe and reason about his or her own present, conscious inner thoughts, sensations, feelings, and soul ... [and] allow for the development of mindfulness, which informs life beyond decontextualized, pre-conceived mindsets" (p. 56). This does not mean that anxiety or fear should direct our actions or inquiries, but emotions should be acknowledged and recognized as possible influences on behavior, and then used to open rather than obstruct learning. Stewart complains that individuals often cut the time for reflection, making it meaningless and he criticizes traditional approaches that reduce reflection to a project management tool. Similarly, Farrell points out that reflection is not a mechanical, mindless task but a multidimensional process involving the whole person.

Reflection in service-learning also involves systematically collecting data about events, behaviors, and interactions in the service experience, as well as from a consideration of aspects beyond the immediate context. Various models, such as Ash et al.'s (2005) DEAL framework, can be used for collecting data. This helps ensure that the reflection is evidence-based (Farrell's second principle).

Engaging in dialogue (third principle) for reflective practice is essential in service-learning. Eyler (2002a), discussing ways to link students and communities, asserts that instructors need to structure opportunities for students to reflect alone, but also with peers and with community partners before, during, and after service. Garrison et al. (2010) suggest ways to develop a "community of inquiry" to promote reflective dialogue in e-service-learning contexts (see Chapter 6). Reflecting together strengthens community, a key aspect of service-learning.

Points for Reflection
- Do you agree that dialogue can promote reflective practice?
- How might you implement dialogue for reflective practice in your TESOL service-learning context?

Farrell's (2019) fourth principle, reflective practice bridges principles and practices, is a key component of service-learning. As discussed earlier, it is the connection between the service experience (practice) and academic work (theory) that defines service-learning approaches. It is through service that learning outcomes are met.

Reflective practice in service-learning also requires an inquiring disposition (Farrell's principle 5). Developing curiosity and asking questions is important for exploring the causes and consequences of events, behaviors, interactions, and experiences. A disposition of inquiry helps participants wonder about how they can improve both their current and future practice. But more than this, a disposition of inquiry can prompt participants to question beliefs and norms, and challenge social injustices. Eyler (2002a) asserts that students "are more likely to develop the capacity for critical thought if they are challenged both by surprising experiences and by reflective teachers who help them explore these experiences and question their fundamental assumptions about their world" (pp. 521–522). Farrell (2019) builds on Dewey (1933) by explaining that encouraging the development of various attitudes can support inquiry and guide reflective practice. The attitudes are open-mindedness, wholeheartedness, directness, and responsibility. These attitudes may overlap with principle 1, being holistic. In TESOL service-learning, we need open-mindedness to question language teaching and learning events, actions, and norms, and to invite alternative perspectives. We need wholeheartedness to foster curiosity and enthusiasm for language teaching and learning and for the service experience. Open-mindedness and wholeheartedness can be brought to discussions to energize the reflective process with others. Directness in service-learning can be considered as a sense of purpose or focus on meeting community needs and learning goals. This requires skills in observation and self-awareness. Directness in reflective practice helps construct meaning from the experience. Responsibility in service-learning builds on this as participants consider impacts on and consequences of events, behaviors, interactions and experiences. By modeling and fostering these attitudes in service-learning, a disposition of inquiry can be nurtured for critical reflection and transformative learning.

Points for Reflection
- How important do you think open-mindedness, wholeheartedness, directness, and responsibility are in reflective practice in TESOL service-learning?
- How might you nurture an inquiring disposition for reflective practice in TESOL service-learning?

This easily leads us to Farrell's (2019) sixth principle: reflective practice is a way of life. After developing a disposition of inquiry, greater self-awareness, civic identity, cognitive, metacognitive, and affective processes, skills in observation and critical reflection during service-learning, it is hoped that participants will continue to engage with their communities and explore their experiences. Continuous reflection can bring awareness and meaning and deeper understanding. It enables continuous improvement in terms of teaching and of civic engagement. It can build confidence and a sense of renewal as beliefs, values, and practices are continually explored. And it can empower participants to work towards a more just world. For example, reflecting on how multilingual learners are treated in the community can empower ESOL teachers to advocate for them.

Points for Reflection
- To what extent do you think that Farrell's six principles of reflective practice in ELT can be applied to reflective practice in TESOL service-learning in your context?

CONCLUSION

This chapter has attempted to characterize reflective practice in TESOL service-learning by drawing on work from Dewey (1910) to Eyler (2002a), Jacoby (2014), Gorski and Dalton (2020), Farrell (2019), and others. By reviewing others' work and asking and addressing questions, and looking at relevant examples, we develop an understanding of reflective practice in a service-learning context. This understanding informs how we can determine the effectiveness of reflections in TESOL service-learning. Ways to analyze and assess reflections are explored in Chapter 3.

Chapter 3

Analyzing and Assessing Reflections in TESOL Service-Learning

INTRODUCTION

Informed by the purpose, characteristics, and principles of reflective practice in service-learning explored in Chapter 2, this chapter focuses on analyzing and assessing reflections in TESOL service-learning and the issues associated with this. In my years as a teacher and teacher educator, I have learned that we should not think about assessment at the end of a linear process where goal setting is the first stage and assessment the last. Rather, assessment should be considered from the beginning, as in "backward design" (Wiggins & McTighe, 1998). It is the same for service-learning, where assessment should be considered together with the goals, outcomes, and objectives when planning the service-learning experience. This is because assessing participants' work and performance (and evaluating the effectiveness of the project) is typically determined by identifying the extent to which service-learning objectives are met. While students' performance and achievement of objectives can be measured in multiple ways through various artifacts, this chapter focuses specifically on assessment of learning through reflections. We will discuss issues of assessing reflections and present various models of how reflections can be assessed.

GOALS, OUTCOMES, AND OBJECTIVES OF TESOL SERVICE-LEARNING

Before elaborating on analysis and assessment of reflections, it is useful to remember that the purpose of reflection is to improve learning, and learning is more likely to occur when a service-learning experience is carefully planned. Planning starts with a consideration of desired goals, outcomes, and objectives. Achieving learning outcomes is one of the key aspects of service-learning identified in most definitions of service-learning. Moreover, achievement of target goals, outcomes, and objectives through service-learning helps validate it as an effective learning method (McGowan, 2017).

Points for Reflection
- How do you distinguish the terms goals, outcomes, and objectives?

Distinguishing the terms, *goals*, *outcomes*, and *objectives* can be problematic, so I would first like to share how I interpret them. For me, a *goal* is a broad purpose or general aim; an *outcome* is a result or benefit from achieving learning objectives; and a learning *objective* is a relevant and specific learning target that is observable, measurable (assessable), and time bound. Outcomes and objectives are similar, but outcomes are the resulting knowledge, skills and dispositions that are gained in the end, while objectives are more specific ways of working towards meeting outcomes. Service-learning goals, outcomes, and objectives may be modified or adopted verbatim from the academic program (TESOL), and supplemented with others that more specifically address the service-learning targets. For example, a broad service-learning goal might be to "develop civic responsibility through service". A service-learning outcome might be that students will "develop leadership and teamwork skills needed for effective community engagement" (University of Southern Indiana, 2020). A specific service-learning objective might be that "participants will be able to demonstrate collaboration strategies when working with partners to support learners in an after-school program". Notice how the focus becomes narrower in the objective. Ash et al. (2005) demonstrated the need for objectives to be specific when they found that their service-learning objectives, "academic enhancement", "civic engagement", and "personal growth", were too vague to adequately assess learning.

In a TESOL service-learning context, a goal might be "academic skills development". An outcome might be an "ability to connect theories of language learning and the service-learning experience". An objective might be to "make language input comprehensible by scaffolding learning using visuals and gestures". Again, the focus narrows from the broad goal to the specific objective.

There are a couple of points to note here. First, the number of TESOL service-learning outcomes and objectives depends on the context and duration of the service-learning as well as the needs of the program or course. Outcomes may not be met or assessed solely through the service-learning experience, so the totality of the course and the program needs to be considered. Also note that outcomes and objectives may apply to more than one goal. Regardless of how the goals, outcomes, and objectives are planned, they should be structured in a way that enables assessment. Outcomes for the community partner should also be planned, but that is beyond the scope of this book. Finally, it is important to note that the development of goals, outcomes, and objectives is not meant to be rigidly prescriptive or restrict aspects of service-learning experiences. The purpose is to provide meaningful guidance to support and enhance learning and the achievement of course goals.

> **Points for Reflection**
> - Consider a TESOL course or program that you teach. How might a service-learning experience enhance learning in your TESOL course/program?
> - What goals, outcomes, and objectives would you design for a TESOL service-learning project in your context?
> - With what tools would you assess the service-learning outcomes and objectives?

As with any effective course planning, when instructors set the goals, outcomes, and objectives for their courses and service-learning projects, they need to concomitantly consider how these will be assessed, that is, how will changes in skills, knowledge, performance, and attitude be measured? It is the specific, observable, measurable, time-bound objectives that will guide the selection of the assessment tools and this will help determine the extent to which the goals, outcomes, and learning objectives have been met. It is possible that outcomes may be introduced or reinforced in a particular TESOL course, but not fully assessed until a later course in the TESOL program. Instructors should be mindful of this as they plan. Clear assessment tools, guidelines, and transparent rubrics should be designed in advance and show alignment between tools and learning objectives of both the community-based and academic-based parts of the course.

FORMATS OF ASSESSMENT IN TESOL SERVICE-LEARNING

Assessment tools in TESOL service-learning, should complement other assessment measures used in the course. Using multiple assessment tools and artifacts can facilitate ongoing assessment that can be both formative and summative, and by employing assessment before, during, and after the community experience, a fairly accurate picture of performance and development can be gained. It is not always possible to directly observe performance in a consistent way; hence, assessment can be indirect. In TESOL service-learning, assessment artifacts might include:

- reflections
- lesson plans and teaching materials
- samples of learner work

- instructor and site-supervisor observation notes and reports
- teaching portfolios
- exit interviews
- self and peer assessment.

Gottlieb and Robinson (2006) point out that it is important to have students self-assess as this builds self-awareness and metacognitive skills, which are typical outcomes of service-learning. Assessment artifacts specifically for self and/or peer assessments might include:

- competency checklists
- peer observation reports
- video self-analysis reports
- progress reports
- pre- and post-experience surveys.

Care should be taken when using assessment tools that require self-reporting, such as surveys, because there is a danger that "self-report as an assessment strategy often confuses student satisfaction with student learning" (Ash et al., 2005, p. 50).

USING REFLECTION TO ASSESS LEARNING IN SERVICE-LEARNING

Jacoby (2014) reminds us that "there can be no service-learning without reflection" (p. 50) and reflection is commonly used for assessment because reflection translates the service-learning experience into knowledge (Cho & Gulley, 2017). Ash et al. (2005) also advocate the use of reflection for learning, stating: "Through guided reflection, students individually and in groups – examine their experiences critically and articulate specific learning outcomes, thus enhancing the quality of their learning and of their service" (p. 51). In other words, by impelling participants to articulate or express what they have learned, reflections can provide evidence of learning. Ward and McCotter (2004) also assert that reflection is meaningful when it focuses on the process of learning, but, importantly, they caution that reflection should not simply be a tool for documenting the achievement of outcomes. Reflection can be so much more as a vehicle to help preservice teachers develop qualities that are valued in education, like critical thinking, curiosity, problem-solving, and metacognition, and regular reflection can encourage ongoing development.

> **Points for Reflection**
> - Why is it important to use multiple reflection tools?
> - In your opinion, how important is self-assessment in reflections?
> - To what extent do you agree with Ward and McCotter (2004) that reflection should not simply be a tool for documenting the achievement of outcomes?

Reflection artifacts can be oral, written, or multimodal, and can comprise multiple formats, such as:

- journal entries/blogs/vlogs
- reflection papers
- presentations
- group discussions
- podcasts
- discussion boards
- role plays
- posters
- performances – songs, skits, plays, puppet shows
- artwork, crafts
- workshops.

For details on some of these artifacts, see Chapter 4. The choice of assessment artifacts should be made intentionally to ensure a match with the objectives. When planning assessment through reflection, there are several questions that instructors need to consider. For example, which learning objectives should be addressed through reflection? How many reflection artifacts should preservice teachers complete for assessment and when should they be submitted? Will the assessments be formative or summative? Which mode and format of reflection artifact would provide the best evidence for the target learning objective to be assessed? Will the reflections build on one another to show development, or be isolated reflections to target particular aspects of the experience? Will preservice teachers reflect individually, in pairs, or as a group, with or without the community partner? How will the reflections be scaffolded, by what criteria will they be assessed, and what percentage of the final TESOL course grade will they be allocated?

ISSUES IN ANALYZING AND ASSESSING REFLECTIONS ON SERVICE-LEARNING

The fact that reflection is a required part of service-learning reinforces the understanding that participants learn through the process of reflection. As Ash and

Clayton (2009) point out (emphasis in the original), reflection "*generates* learning (articulating questions, confronting bias, examining causality, contrasting theory with practice, pointing to systemic issues), *deepens* learning (challenging simplistic conclusions, inviting alternative perspectives, asking 'why' iteratively), and *documents* learning (producing tangible expressions of new understandings for evaluation)" (p. 27). Reflecting on service-learning can be a transformative learning experience because it can change the way individuals see the world as they develop their critical thinking, problem-solving, metacognition, social and personal awareness, sense of civic responsibility, and so on (Eyler et al. 1996). Nevertheless, learning is not guaranteed and not all reflections demonstrate learning – even if learning *has* occurred. Molee et al. (2010) make the point that "[d]espite its centrality, reflection is perhaps the most challenging aspect of service-learning to assess" (p. 240). Perhaps unsurprisingly, research studies on assessment of learning through reflection in service-learning contexts are limited and reveal mixed results. Despite the potential to transform learning, various challenges emerge when assessing reflective practice in service-learning.

In reflections that they examined, Ash et al. (2005) found there was a "disconnect between what the students were learning and what we had hoped they would learn" (p. 52) during service-learning, particularly in terms of demonstrating understanding the application of course content, hence they developed their DEAL model (see Chapter 2). The failure to link academic learning gained from coursework with the experience is a common problem, particularly if students are unaware that this is expected. It is also common to find that reflections do not demonstrate any significant sense of how the experience has impacted the preservice teachers' awareness of their own learning. These problems in reflections – lack of academic and service-learning connection and lack of metacognition – can be overcome with clear guidelines and transparent expectations.

Another problem that Ash and Clayton (2009) note is the lack of depth in reflections and overgeneralizations. Following up on this, Molee et al. (2010) conducted their own study to evaluate the DEAL model (Ash & Clayton, 2009) for assessing student learning through critical reflections. Their findings show that "the depth of learning scores for the majority of students fell into the categories of lower-order thinking skills (identify, describe, and apply) and their critical thinking ranged from poor to fair" (p. 250). Similarly, McGowan (2017) and others (Eyler et al. 1996) assert that, typically, there is a range in quality of reflections in service-learning. High order cognitive skills, like self-awareness, critical thinking, metacognition, open-mindedness – usually associated with evidence of learning – are required in effective reflection (Coulson & Harvey, 2012); yet, despite efforts to clarify expectations, reflections can be superficial and uncritical, focusing too much on descriptions of what students did or observed and how they felt.

What makes reflection in TESOL service-learning distinctive is the opportunity for TESOL students to reflect, not just on the theory and principles of language learning and ELT in practice as they develop their academic and professional skills in the community, but also on their personal and social development, including their sense of civic responsibility as they engage with linguistically and culturally diverse learners and community partners. In effective service-learning projects, all participants should have agency, so the power differential should be less marked than in a teaching practicum. It is hoped, therefore, that participants would feel free to reflect candidly. Given the nature of our field where we work with diverse populations, preservice teachers are encouraged to challenge assumptions and beliefs and, in some contexts, reflect critically on important social justice issues of both local and broader concern, such as diversity, equity, and inclusion, multiculturalism and multilingualism, translanguaging, racism, stereotyping, language and education policies, immigration, access to services, how to advocate for ELs, among other things. Yet, these aspects are not often considered in reflections for various reasons. Sometimes, the goals and expectations may not be transparent, or preservice students are not prepared or have not yet developed the capacity for greater criticality. Often, preservice teachers feel uncomfortable reflecting critically, and sometimes institutional or cultural constraints limit this type of reflection. For more on critical reflection, see Chapter 2. In my own context, I have found that, without raising awareness of such issues, many preservice ESOL teachers reflect exclusively on the personal and affective aspects of the service-learning experience. They describe their general joy, frustration, or confidence level in working with ELs, but do not display any deeper thinking about the causes of specific incidents or critical analysis of injustices that impact multilingual learners.

This is not to say that feelings are not important in reflections. Indeed, affective learning cannot be ignored, as Dewey (1933), Farrell (2019), Kiely (2005), Stewart (2011), and others have shown. Given that emotions are part of the reflection process, other problems can arise. Some students may have difficulties trying to intellectualize and articulate feelings of guilt or despair or surprise or empathy experienced during service-learning, yet such feelings imply a transformation as part of the learning process. Moreover, it is much easier to measure the acquisition of knowledge than it is to measure the development of empathy through reflective practice. Jacoby (2014) addresses this point when she asserts that "we should not assess or grade the content of students' feelings. Rather, we should assess how authentically and deeply students think about their feelings" (p. 40). We will return to this issue of affective learning later.

These issues suggest that "[a] large part of the 'learning' in service-learning is the enhancement of reflective judgment" and "educators who prepare students for service-learning must help students enhance their level of reflective judgment" (Averett

& Arnd-Caddigan, 2014, p. 319). Yet, this raises more questions. How can reflections be effective representations of learning? Do all participants have the capacity to reflect effectively? Can reflection be taught? Are instructors prepared to teach or scaffold reflective thinking? How can reflections be analyzed and assessed? Indeed, should reflections be assessed? Reflections should be honest and personally meaningful in order to promote learning and foster growth, but if reflections are assessed as a requirement for coursework, how personal and how honest will they be? Might some preservice ESOL teachers simply follow the educator's guidelines for reflection assignments and reflect – not in any personally meaningful way – but in a way that will simply meet the requirements and expectations. In other words, will students submit reflections on what the instructor wants to hear rather than what preservice teachers actually think or feel? Related to this, Farrell (2019) cautions that reflection should not become a mechanical procedure for approaching teaching and learning. How can reflections foster growth if they are perceived as simply an academic exercise?

Points for Reflection
- In what ways do you think reflections might represent learning?
- In your view, does everyone have the capacity to reflect effectively?
- Can reflection be taught? How might you teach or scaffold reflective thinking in your context?
- Do you believe that reflections in TESOL service-learning should be assessed?
- In your context, how honest or sincere do you think preservice ESOL teachers would be in their reflections?

To begin addressing some of the issues, it is helpful to remember that service-learning is defined as:

> a course or competency-based, credit-bearing educational experience in which students (a) participate in mutually identified service activities that benefit the community, and (b) reflect on the service activity in such a way as to gain further understanding of course content, a broader appreciation of the discipline, and an enhanced sense of personal values and civic responsibility. (Bringle & Clayton, 2012, p. 105)

The credit-bearing aspect of service-learning and the requirement to meet selected course objectives during the engagement with the community partner means that assessing service-learning is required. The duration of the service-learning project – whether a single lesson or a whole semester or something in between – will dictate the type and amount of assessment that is used. On-site observations by the instructor or community partner, as well as assessment of lesson plans and teaching materials, may be used to demonstrate professional and social development, but greater insight, especially into metacognition and personal growth, can be gained through reflections. It is reflection that compels participants to connect the community engagement to the academic learning and, knowing that reflection is a crucial part of service-learning, it is reasonable to expect that reflection should form part (or sometimes all) of the service-learning assessment. As such, it is essential to discuss with preservice teachers the importance of reflection in service-learning, the expectations for reflections, and details of how the reflections will be assessed. Assessment guidelines and rubrics can be designed in a way that allows individual style and content preferences while still meeting objectives and this needs to be understood by everyone. Examples can be shared with preservice teachers to demonstrate how objectives and expectations can be met (and not met), as well as how and where there is flexibility in style. If participants understand the benefits to their learning, it is more likely they will reflect honestly.

MODELS FOR ANALYZING REFLECTIONS

Despite considerable research showing positive educational results for service-learning (Ash & Clayton, 2009; Barnes & Caprino, 2016; Bringle & Clayton, 2020; Burke et al, 2021; Cho & Gulley, 2017; Eyler, 2000; Felten & Clayton, 2011; Furco et al., 2010; Hatcher & Bringle, 1997), there have been some questions about a lack of assessment transparency and dependence on self-reporting. This has resulted in calls over the years to advance the validity of service-learning as a teaching and learning approach by demonstrating achievement of academic and cognitive outcomes (Eyler, 2000; Furco et al., 2010; Molee et al., 2010; McGowan, 2017; Hicks et al., 2019). In response, self-reporting measures have generally been replaced by more robust forms of reflection assessments, and various models of analysis have been used in service-learning to demonstrate how reflections provide evidence of learning. Nevertheless, results of studies determining achievement of outcomes through service-learning have been inconsistent for various reasons. Molee et al. (2010) point out that there is sometimes a conflation of participant satisfaction with student learning, as well as variability in the quality of the experiences due to flexibility in service-learning formats. McGowan (2017) claims that there is often a focus on evaluating program effectiveness rather than student learning, as well as a lack of systematic and rigorous tools to evaluate learning. Hicks et al. (2019) add that research on the quality of critical reflection is sparse. Consequently, the need to demonstrate learning and share effective models for analyzing reflections remains important. Most models used in service-learning have been informed by reflective practice in teacher education and other fields. Useful descriptions of various models in education and ELT are presented in Ward and McCotter (2004) and Farrell (2019, pp. 21–27).

Models used for analyzing reflections in service-learning vary in context, structure, and focus. For example, many models comprise a simple three/five-level framework. Others involve integrating levels with various dimensions. Some models specifically target critical reflection, while others do not. Selected models of reflection are summarized in Table 3.1.

I would like to highlight a few points about some of the models presented in Table 3.1. Bradley's (1995) model for analyzing reflections was originally applied in an economics service-learning course, but has since been applied in other disciplines. The model uses a three-factor scoring system:

- *Level one reflections* present descriptions of observations with examples, but they are simple without insight into reasons for situations. Beliefs at this level are personal and unsupported. Ideas may be repeated from those discussed in class.
- *Level two reflections* present more thorough observations with some nuance and clear critique from one perspective without consideration of the broader context. Differences of viewpoint are perceived and there is some ability to provide and interpret evidence.
- *Level three* reflections demonstrate an ability to see multiple perspectives, view complexity of situations in the broader context, and make objective judgments based on reasoning and evidence. There is also insight into the impact of decisions at this level.

Jacoby (2014) characterizes the three levels as "surface", "emerging", and "deep" (p. 41). Limiting the model to three levels is attractive for many instructors because of its simplicity. Importantly, Bradley (1995) stresses the formative nature of assessing reflections and advises that "the factors should not be consolidated into a single grade as the measurement is not quantitative – the numbers used are ranks, not quantities" (p. 20). He also points out that "a single journal excerpt is unlikely to show all of the items listed as characterizing a particular level. Rather they serve as typical representatives of thinking at each level" (p. 21) and assigning levels should be accompanied by a verbal explanation of why the particular level was selected. These points are important because they demonstrate complexities in assessing reflection.

Similar three- to five-level structures are used in other models for analyzing service-learning reflections, such as Smit and Tremethick (2017) and Terry and Bohnenberger (2004). Other models involve more complexity by mapping different levels to multiple dimensions, or applied to existing taxonomies (Ash & Clayton,

Table 3.1. Models for analyzing reflections

Authors	Context	Model structure and focus
Ash & Clayton (2004, 2009), Ash, Clayton & Atkinson (2005)	Critical reflection in service-learning USA	DEAL framework of questions (3 processes): describe, examine, articulate learning Multiple rubrics for 3 dimensions: academic enhancement, civic learning, and personal growth mapped against various criteria modified from Bloom's (1956) taxonomy and Paul & Elder's (2001) critical thinking standards
Averett & Arnd-Caddigan (2014)	Service-learning in social work USA	Application of King & Kitchener's (2004) "Judgment Model": 3 levels – "pre-reflective thinking", "quasi-reflective thinking", "reflective thinking" – mapped onto 7 stages based on theories of knowledge. Not necessarily linear
Barnes & Caprino (2016)	Critical reflection in service-learning USA	Application of Fink's (2013) taxonomy of six categories: "foundational knowledge", "application", "integration", "human dimension", "caring", and "learning how to learn". Non-linear
Bradley (1995)	Service-learning in economics USA	3 levels, labelled by Jacoby (2014) as "surface", "emerging", and "deep"
Gorski & Dalton (2020)	Multicultural and social justice teacher education USA	5 levels: "Amorphous cultural reflection", "Personal identity reflection", "Cultural competence reflection", "Equitable and just school reflection", "School transformation reflection". Categorized as "conservative", "liberal", or "critical"
Kiely (2005)	Service-learning program in Nicaragua	Expansion of Mezirow's (2000) Transformation Theory of Adult Learning 5 dimensions: "contextual border crossing", "dissonance", "personalizing", "processing", "connecting". Critical and transformative focus
Smit & Tremethick (2017)	Service-learning program in Honduras for nursing students	4 levels: "nonreflection", "understanding", "reflection", "critical reflection"
Terry & Bohnenberger (2004)	Service-learning USA	3 levels: "observation", "analysis", "synthesis"
Ward & McCotter (2004)	Critical reflection in teacher education USA	4 levels: "routine", "technical", "dialogic", and "transformative". Mapped to 3 dimensions: "focus on concerns", "process of inquiry", and "change due to inquiry"
Wu & Dahlgren (2011)	TESOL service-learning USA	An application of Gee's (2005) Discourse Analysis – codes reflection transcripts for linguistic and cultural meanings that reflect aspects such as identity and beliefs

2009; Averett & Arnd-Caddigan, 2014; Barnes & Caprino, 2016; Gorski & Dalton, 2020).

Ash and Clayton (2009) recommend drawing on Bloom's (1956) taxonomy and Paul and Elder's (2001) critical thinking standards to create rubrics for analyzing reflections at the three stages of their DEAL model. They map the stages to three goal categories: academic enhancement, civic learning, and personal growth. The authors state that the assessment approach can be formative as well as summative. The "learning objectives and critical thinking guide are tools to be used by the students to help focus and deepen their reflective thinking" (Ash et al., 2005, p. 52), and a cyclical process of reflection and feedback is implemented over the semester. See more of the DEAL model in the "Assessing and Giving Feedback on TESOL Service-learning Reflections" section later in this chapter.

Wu and Dahlgren (2011) applied Gee's (2005) discourse analysis to investigate oral reflection interviews in a TESOL service-learning context to "see how student learners critically reflect on the social realities of immigrants" (p. 271). Analyzing reflections for linguistic and cultural meanings in this way makes interesting research; however, discourse analysis is likely too time-consuming for TESOL instructors to use in education contexts.

Points for Reflection

- Consider the type of model you might use to analyze reflections in service-learning. Would a three-level model be appropriate for identifying targeted learning according to the goals and objectives, or would you use a more complex model?
- How might you adapt an existing model to suit your needs?

Before discussing assessment of reflections, I would like to mention two models that focus on critical reflection for transformative learning. The first is Gorski and Dalton's (2020) model, used in multicultural education. Their model may be of interest to TESOL instructors who encourage a social justice approach to critical reflection. The authors support transformative learning and working towards addressing injustices through critical reflection. Importantly, however, Gorski and Dalton stress that reflections that do not demonstrate criticality are not indicative of a lack of critical reflection in a course. They are also careful to advise that their model is not to be used to critique instructors or as a push to dismiss reflections that are not considered critical. Their point "is not to advocate for a diminished presence of non-critical reflection, but rather for a greater presence of critical reflection" (p. 366). In other words, instructors must determine the purpose of the reflections and other assignments in meeting the needs for evidence of learning or meeting identified objectives.

The second model was created by Kiely (2005) to address his concern that research on service-learning does not often reveal a "transformative impact on students' moral, political, intellectual, personal, cultural, and spiritual perspectives" (p. 6), particularly when service-learning:

> provides students with opportunities to explore the meaning of global citizenship to help students learn to question unjust social, political, economic, and cultural norms, institutions, and policies, and to engage in social action to transform institutions and policies that perpetuate social injustice, political oppression, and economic disparities locally and globally. (p. 7)

While Kiely (2005) acknowledges the value of reflection in the learning process, he asserts that contextual factors and non-reflective forms of learning have been neglected. With his model, he suggests linking critical reflection with affective learning over time. He also stresses the importance of dialogue for gaining diverse perspectives, building empathy, and helping students question dominant cultural norms, ideologies and assumptions related to civic mindedness and social justice. I agree that reflective dialogue gives participants opportunities to express and explore feelings together and demonstrate learning through reflection with others. Peers and instructors can provide formative feedback to help guide further reflection.

Kiely (2005) also claims that "transformational learning is more apt to occur and persist over the long-term if there are structured opportunities for participants to engage in reflective (i.e., processing) and nonreflective (i.e., personalizing and connecting) learning processes with peers, faculty, and community members" (p. 17). Since Kiely's publication, Stewart (2011), Jacoby (2014) and others have acknowledged the importance of affect in service-learning, and, accordingly, building affect into the service-learning outcomes and reflective practice is essential. In TESOL service-learning, affective learning is related to such things as developing empathy, openness to others' perspectives, cultural sensitivity, sense of civic responsibility.

I question Kiely's (2005) use of the term "nonreflective" processes, because I view affective learning and empathizing and connecting as *part of* the reflective process. Admittedly, some educators may not agree with Kiely that skits, singing, dancing, or artwork, poetry, or posters are representative of reflective practice, yet, what is happening in students' heads and hearts can sometimes emerge through such actions more clearly than through written or verbal reflections. Indeed, the NYLC (2007) includes in its list of reflection activities: murals, musical displays, posters, visual representations, skits or dance that explain perceptions, and Jacoby (2014) includes media and artistic creations, like collective collages, image enhanced essays, and musical compositions as a type of reflection in service-learning. I can share an example of an alternative form of reflection from a service-learning project in my TESOL course. Two of the preservice teachers in the course together designed and taught an after-school lesson for young ELs on the topic of community homelessness. They had a short text on the issue and how important socks were for this population. To motivate the ELs and emphasize the issue, the preservice teachers used sock puppets in their teaching activities. Their written reflections on the experience did not articulate their learning as strongly as they might have, but clearly, these two preservice teachers valued the experience because, a few weeks later, on their own initiative, they organized a free sock-puppet-making workshop for the ELs and their families. They had contacted a local coffee shop and been granted permission to run the workshop there on a Saturday, thus supporting these families and showing them that they are part of the broader community. The preservice teachers' actions demonstrated their strong feelings about the need for such community activities to strengthen community. Though not a traditional reflection artifact, this is clear evidence that these preservice teachers view "community engagement as a positive learning experience" and have developed "a sense of civic identity and commitment to community engagement – two of the service-learning outcomes for the course. Rather than labelling this as nonreflective practice, therefore, I would suggest that it is just a different way to reflect.

A takeaway from exploring different models is that they should be considered in terms of the specific context of use. There is no single best model for analyzing reflections; so, when selecting a model, consider purpose and specific needs and make modifications to align with the goals, outcomes, and objectives of the target service-learning context.

Points for Reflection

- To what extent do you agree with Kiely (2005) that building affect into reflections on service-learning is important?
- What do you think about using artwork and performance as reflection for learning in TESOL service-learning contexts?

ASSESSING REFLECTION TASKS

To assess reflections in a service-learning context, it is important to include a variety of reflection tasks because relying on one or two reflection artifacts would not accurately capture enough information to make a fair assessment. While formative assessment can lead to continuous reflection and broadening perspectives (Ash & Clayton, 2009; Barnes & Caprino, 2016; Gorski & Dalton, 2020; Kiely, 2005), we should keep in mind that time is needed to engage in the reflective process and reach a new level of understanding and transformative learning. In fact, a change in learning may not occur during a single service-learning project. Ward and Mc-Cotter (2004) claim that true transformative learning from reflecting on teaching may not occur within a single semester, or even a year (p. 253). Something else to remember is that service-learning reflections do not account for the full range of learning in a course.

To help facilitate learning, I have found the following steps useful in planning the assessment of reflections:

1. Consider the service-learning goals, outcomes, and objectives, and determine the type of "critical" reflection that is appropriate for the context.
2. List all the planned reflection tasks and identify a related product or artifact that will demonstrate learning, e.g. weekly journal entries, recording (or field notes) of a dialogue, audio or video recordings of reflections, self/peer assessment forms, written reflection papers, multimodal presentations.
3. For each reflection artifact, determine the purpose: what it is that students are meant to learn and demonstrate. These should align with the goals, outcomes, and objectives of the service-learning work. The purpose might directly address a specific learning objective, or it might target a particular need, like developing skills in identifying or analyzing meaningful events, or developing critical awareness, or metacognition. If there is no clear purpose, reconsider using the reflection task.
4. Determine if the reflections will be assessed formatively or summatively.
   (a) Provide opportunities for multiple cycles of reflection and feedback for formative assessment. Some reflection tasks and artifacts may not be assessed at all if they are for participants to practice independently. Others may be given formative oral or written feedback from peers and/or instructor, and some may be self-assessed. If reflection tasks or artifacts are scored, a simple scale may be applied to demonstrate progress, or they may be given a completion mark only.
   (b) Summative reflection artifacts can target specific knowledge, skills and attitudes developed, or include a broader culmination of learning in terms of academic/cognitive, professional, social/civic, and personal development. Affective learning can be included in the social and personal categories.
5. Design the assessment criteria. For validity, careful consideration needs to be taken to align the criteria with the reflection artifact and the purpose. Informed by various models for analyzing reflections, create a clear rubric that will guide assessment of the reflection and provide transparency of expectations for students. Applying a rubric of consistent criteria adds reliability.

6.   Allocate weightages that award most points to tasks and artifacts that require most effort and display most learning.

If instructors decide to assess actions and artifacts, like artwork, theatre, dance, and workshops summatively, they could award extra credit, or build the action into the final assignment as one of the options, for example, I typically give preservice teachers a choice of writing a final reflection paper, or creating a multimodal presentation, or engaging in some approved action, like designing and implementing a community workshop. To increase reliability, the action could be supplemented with a form for self-evaluation or evaluation by a community partner.

ASSESSING AND GIVING FEEDBACK ON TESOL SERVICE-LEARNING REFLECTIONS

When assessing reflections, typically, meaningful chunks are identified that demonstrate evidence of a target criterion. Expectations and rubrics would need to have been shared and modeled in advance. Without guidance, participants may know that their reflections must reflect their learning, but they may limit their reflection to something like this: *I learned how to make it easier for each of the ELs and how to work with each EL one on one.* While this comment explicitly states that learning took place, the lack of specifics in this reflection do not make it very meaningful. This reflection illustrates the need to provide frequent opportunities for reflection and feedback. When providing feedback, it is important to honor the participants' words and try not to interpret them in unintended ways. Prompts can be provided, however, to encourage deeper reflection. In the example above, I might ask the following questions: Did you notice a specific difficulty that an EL faced, or were the difficulties common to all? Why do you think the ELs were experiencing difficulty with the task? Can you give some examples of how you made the task easier for ELs? How do you know you made the task easier? Was working one-on-one helpful? Why/why not? (How) will this experience change your practice in the future? Do you think the ELs face similar challenges in other contexts (in school/outside of school)? Why/Why not? I have also found it useful to reiterate to preservice teachers that specific examples are required to support claims and demonstrate evidence of learning.

Self and peer evaluations can be effective for developing metacognition and self-awareness, which can strengthen reflection skills. Peer evaluation has the added benefit that individuals learn from each other's ideas and perspectives. This doesn't mean, however, that anything goes. Brookfield (1995) asserts that "[s]elf-evaluation that asks for no confirmatory evidence or detailed documentation of the claims students make is intellectually sloppy. It removes from students the obligation to communicate what and how they have learned in clear and verifiable terms" (p. 102). As such, instructors should make it clear in their expectations for self and peer assessments of reflections that evidence and specific examples are required to support claims. In addition, we cannot assume that everyone knows how to conduct a self or peer assessment of reflections or give useful feedback, so training should be provided. Possible prompts for self and peer assessment of reflections are presented below, but these should be customized to the specific type and purpose of the reflection.

Content of the reflection:

- Is a specific event/interaction/experience well selected in terms of significance for learning?
- Is the event/interaction/experience examined or interpreted or analyzed in a credible way?
- Are root causes/responses/alternative responses suggested?
- Does the author demonstrate curiosity? Are additional questions or issues raised?
- Does the author demonstrate self-awareness?
- Does the author challenge beliefs or norms?
- Are conclusions suggested?
- Are implications presented?
- Are suggestions given for making improvements in the future?

Writing of the reflection:

- Are descriptions and explanations clear (coherent and sufficiently developed)?
- Are claims well supported with specific examples or relevant evidence?
- Is the reflection well organized (cohesive)?

Additional comments: When assigning self or peer assessment, it is important to caution participants that, if the reflection focuses on personal feelings, we should not judge the feelings, but rather assess the quality of the thinking.

Finally, if grades help to motivate individuals, completion points or a criteria-based score can be awarded for both the reflection and for the feedback.

Points for Reflection
- What tools do you currently use to assess reflections?
- In your context, how might prompts for summative reflections be different from those used for formative reflections in service-learning?
- What might be some advantages and disadvantages of assessing peer feedback on reflections?

Informed by the DEAL model, yet needing to customize my analysis of final reflections in my TESOL service-learning context to meet the objectives, and assess them in a relatively quick and efficient way, I developed my own assessment rubric. It is presented in Table 3.2.

Based on the sample rubric in Table 3.2, critical reflection in terms of challenging norms, and pursuing social justice issues may be evident at both the "Examination" stage ("Identifies credible influencing factors & related issues – may or may not explore broader ideological issues", and "Considers multiple perspectives on issues to uncover root causes of problems"), as well as in the "Articulated Learning" stage ("Convincingly articulates how beliefs about ELT have changed or been confirmed").

Additional columns of descriptors may be added to allow greater differentiation between levels of reflections. Also note that the four categories may be weighted differently depending on course goals.

> **Points for Reflection**
> - How easy or difficult do you think it might be to use a rubric like the sample in Table 3.2 to assess reflections in TESOL service-learning?
> - How might you modify the rubric for your context?

Normally, I try to provide choices of mode (written, oral, multimodal) for reflections. See my sample final assignment guidelines showing options in Chapter 6. The final reflection would account for a portion of the full assessment of the service-learning experience. Other reflection tasks, such as journal entries, pre and post competency surveys, peer/self-assessments may also be counted.

CONCLUSION

This chapter asked the following questions that can arise when facilitating reflections in service-learning:

- How can reflections be effective representations of learning?
- Do all participants have the capacity to reflect effectively?
- Can reflection be taught?
- Are instructors prepared to teach or scaffold reflective thinking?
- How can reflections in TESOL service-learning be analyzed and assessed?
- Should reflections be assessed?
- Will participants submit reflections on what the instructor wants to hear rather than what they actually think or feel?

Table 3.2. Sample rubric for final reflection on TESOL service-learning experience

DEAL stages	Above expectations	Meets expectations	Approaches expectations
Description of TESOL service-learning experience/ event/ interaction 15%	• Strategically selects meaningful TESOL service-learning events/ interactions/observations – both positive & negative • Describes observations clearly & succinctly with appropriate level of specificity & elaboration	• Selects meaningful TESOL service-learning events/interactions/ observations – both negative & positive • Generally describes observations clearly	• Attempts to select meaningful TESOL service-learning events, interactions, or observations • Attempts to describe observations clearly
Examination (& analysis) of TESOL service-learning experience 40%	• Credibly (with evidence) & insightfully analyzes TESOL service-learning events or observations • Makes relevant links to language learning theory & beliefs about EL teaching/learning • Considers multiple perspectives on issues to uncover root causes of problems • Identifies credible influencing factors & related issues – may or may not explore broader ideological issues	• Analyzes TESOL service-learning events or observations adequately • Explores links to language learning theory &/or beliefs about EL teaching/learning • Attempts to uncover root causes of problems • Suggests influencing factors &/or related issues	• Attempts to analyze TESOL service-learning events or observations • Refers to language learning theory &/or beliefs about EL teaching/ learning with some inaccuracy • May attempt to uncover root causes of problems but with limited credibility • May suggest influencing factors &/ or related issues but with limited credibility

Articulated Learning 40%	• Demonstrates self-awareness by identifying, with justification, strengths & weaknesses in ELT skills that emerged in service-learning experience • Suggests credible plans for improving practice • Convincingly articulates how beliefs about ELT have changed or been confirmed • Identifies credible examples of how community engagement affects self	• Identifies strengths & weaknesses in ELT skills with some justification • Suggests plans for improving practice • Articulates how beliefs about ELT have changed or been confirmed • Identifies examples of how community engagement affects self	• Attempts to identify relevant strengths & weaknesses in ELT skills • Suggests plans for improving practice, but they may lack credibility • May or may not articulate how beliefs about ELT have changed or been confirmed • May or may not identify examples of how community engagement affects self
Formatting (if applicable) 5%	• Uses appropriate language for the context • Follows accurate APA formatting conventions • Presents information clearly and cohesively	• Generally uses appropriate language for the context • Generally follows accurate APA formatting conventions • Presents information clearly & cohesively for the most part	• Attempts to use appropriate language for the context • May or may not follow APA formatting conventions • Attempts to present information clearly

Answers to the questions depend on the context, but in general, reflections can provide evidence of learning when they display understanding with credible and well-supported claims that align to target goals and objectives. Some participants will reflect more effectively than others, but my experience has shown that sharing a clear purpose for reflection, along with expectations and guidance, helps all participants develop reflection skills. Although we cannot necessarily "teach" dispositions needed for reflection, like curiosity, metacognition, and criticality, we can share tools and models that help develop them. As instructors, we can read, talk to colleagues, attend training and conferences to continually learn about models and techniques to scaffold reflective thinking. There is no prescribed model for analyzing and assessing reflections, so instructors should use what works in their context for their target goals. Reflection is a key component of service-learning and should be assessed, both formatively and summatively, to send the message that reflective practice is important. When relevant feedback is provided and acted upon, it can help participants further develop their reflection skills and see how reflective practice can benefit them in multiple ways, not just to meet goals in their current studies, but into their futures as well.

To encourage participants to be honest and sincere in their reflections, it helps to set up a community of learners where everyone feels safe expressing their thoughts. Guidance and expectations should be clear, but content and style of reflections should not be prescribed, so participants have space to be personal and creative. With multiple opportunities to reflect formally and informally, in multiple formats, there is more likelihood that reflections will be sincere and meaningful. Tools and strategies for facilitating effective reflections are presented and discussed in Chapter 4.

Chapter 4

Facilitating Reflective Practice in TESOL Service-Learning

INTRODUCTION

As a child, were you ever told to go to your room or a time-out corner to "think about your behavior"? For some, this may have been an effective way to compel reflection and change future behavior, but, usually, we cannot force someone to successfully reflect on their experience if they do not want to or do not know how. Brookfield (1995) points out that it is tremendously difficult for anyone, even when making a conscious effort, to escape their own assumptions or taken-for-granted beliefs, and ways of thinking. I remember myself as a child thinking, "I didn't do anything!" I could not get past my assumption that, whatever it was, it was someone else's fault. Of course, as an adult I know that I should be aware of my own assumptions and reflect on issues with an open and critical mind, but even with the benefit of age and this awareness, it can be difficult. Undoubtedly reflection can be challenging for preservice ESOL teachers in service-learning as well. Simply asking them to reflect on their actions does not generally result in meaningful reflection. It is for this reason that Leeuwen et al. (2017) echo Schön (1987) and others when they assert that "[t]rue reflective practice requires the guidance of a mentor or professional supervisor who can ask appropriate questions to ensure that the reflective process is productive and then acted upon" (p. 131).

In previous chapters, we discussed the importance of reflective practice in service-learning, characteristics of reflections, models for analyzing reflections, and insights we can gain from them. We reviewed the benefits of reflection in service-learning and understand that reflective practice has the potential to deepen understandings, build self-awareness, and, through dialogue with others, open our minds and help us develop academically/cognitively, professionally, socially/civically, and personally. So how can reflection in TESOL service-learning help in achieving these outcomes? It is not without its challenges, as discussed in Chapter 3. Can instructors "teach" an attitude or disposition of inquiry that leads to reflection? How can instructors create mandatory academic reflection assignments in TESOL service-learning that lead to learning? How can reflective practice be cultivated so that it becomes a natural process/action for ESOL teachers and not just an added burden for overworked teachers? These are the issues discussed in this chapter. Spoiler alert: there are no easy answers or solutions offered here. The good news is that reflective practice can be facilitated in ways that promote individual and community development.

One of the questions raised was whether or not it was possible to teach a disposition of inquiry and the ability to reflect in a meaningful way. While it may not be possible to "teach" a disposition or attitude, I believe that dispositions can be nurtured by providing tools and strategies, and by modelling reflective practice and demonstrating the benefits. In addition, multiple studies (Ash & Clayton, 2005; Barnes & Caprino, 2016; Bradley, 1995; Jacoby, 2014) in service-learning have found that, to increase the likelihood of more insightful and meaningful reflection, the purpose and expectations must be clear, and instructors must provide guidance, as well as frequent opportunities for preservice ESOL teachers to reflect and get feedback.

This chapter offers a variety of tools and strategies that can be used to facilitate reflective practice in TESOL service-learning contexts. Reflection is expected at multiple stages of the service-learning experience, so useful tools and strategies for facilitating meaningful reflection before, during, and after the service-learning experience are presented. The purpose of sharing these tools is not to prescribe a best way, but rather to offer suggestions for readers to consider and adapt for their context. Different modes of reflection are discussed – oral and written, formal and informal – and various formats of reflection are suggested, such as group and class discussions, oral debriefings, reflection journals, and reflection papers. Multimodal reflections are mentioned here, though more attention is given to these in Chapter 6. The chapter ends with a look at tools and strategies for assessing reflections in this context.

GENERAL STRATEGIES FOR FACILITATING REFLECTIVE PRACTICE IN TESOL SERVICE-LEARNING

Eyler (2002a) asserts that "students are unlikely to engage in reflection on their community placements unless intentional efforts are taken to make it so" (p. 522). As instructors think about facilitating reflective practice in service-learning, it helps to recall the NYLC (2008) reflection standard and indicators and plan accordingly. These are listed below and will be referred to throughout this chapter.

NYLC Service-learning Reflection Standard and Indicators:

1. Service-learning reflection includes a variety of verbal, written, artistic, and nonverbal activities to demonstrate understanding and changes in participants' knowledge, skills, and/or attitudes.
2. Service-learning reflection occurs before, during, and after the service experience.
3. Service-learning reflection prompts participants to think deeply about complex community problems and alternative solutions.
4. Service-learning reflection encourages participants to examine their preconceptions and assumptions in order to explore and understand their roles and responsibilities as citizens.
5. Service-learning reflection encourages participants to examine a variety of social and civic issues related to their service-learning experience so that participants understand connections to public policy and civic life.

Informed by these reflection standard indicators, I present eight general strategies to facilitate reflective practice in TESOL service-learning courses:

1. Share course outline, service-learning goals and objectives, and assessment details early.
2. Foster a sense of curiosity.
3. Ensure understanding of the meaning of service-learning, including reflective practice.
4. Prepare preservice teachers for reflection in TESOL service-learning.
5. Engage preservice teachers in reflection BEFORE service-learning.
6. Engage preservice teachers in reflection DURING service-learning.
7. Engage preservice teachers in reflection AFTER service-learning.
8. Monitor and provide feedback throughout.

These strategies are explained below in the context of TESOL service-learning.

SHARE COURSE OUTLINE, SERVICE-LEARNING GOALS AND OBJECTIVES, ASSESSMENT DETAILS

At the beginning of any course, it is important to make the course outline, learning objectives, assessment process, and assignments clear. Service-learning may be new to some individuals, so how the service-learning goals and objectives fit into the course also need to be explained. This can be done through lecture or simply by providing a detailed syllabus to preservice ESOL teachers. In my courses, I conduct a "syllabus scavenger hunt". Individually or in groups preservice ESOL teachers must find targeted items (answers to specific questions) in the syllabus. For example, instructions might be to find four service-learning objectives, an assignment that is worth 30%, the dates for the service-learning experience, and so on. This is followed with a class discussion to ensure that the learning objectives and assignments are understood. As reflections form part of the assessment, it can be a good idea to highlight this, and opportunities should be provided for deeper discussion and practice later. Asking participants to create a calendar of service-learning assignments can also be a good idea.

FOSTER A SENSE OF CURIOSITY

In my TESOL courses, I start by trying to foster in preservice ESOL teachers a sense of curiosity about what service-learning is. To this end, I show photos and artifacts from previous service-learning experiences (having obtained permission first). This makes the concept of service-learning a little more concrete and demonstrates achievable outcomes. We are fortunate to have an ongoing collaborative partnership with a local elementary school where we organize an after-school literacy program to support young ELs. The preservice ESOL teachers plan and deliver the literacy sessions, and at the end, they compile photos, samples of ELs' work, and personalized motivational comments on the ELs' progress to create a booklet that each participant receives. The booklet becomes a meaningful souvenir of the experience for the participants. When new cohorts of preservice ESOL teachers view these booklets, they often have numerous questions. Their questions here demonstrate curiosity and mark the start of their reflective process. This sense of curiosity needs to be fostered throughout the service-learning experience. Instructors can help by raising issues, posing questions, and providing reflection prompts.

Points for Reflection
- If you have conducted (TESOL) service-learning in the past, how did you communicate the importance of service-learning and of reflective practice to preservice teachers?
- How can instructors ensure that they and the preservice teachers they teach share an understanding of reflective practice?

ENSURE UNDERSTANDING OF THE MEANING OF SERVICE-LEARNING, INCLUDING REFLECTIVE PRACTICE

Preservice ESOL teachers need to be prepared for the service-learning experience and for reflective practice. This involves coming to a shared understanding of what service-learning is. An early class discussion provides diagnostic information about the preservice teachers' familiarity with service-learning and reflective practice. Although it is intended to be an exploratory discussion, using specific prompts to guide the discussion can produce responses with useful diagnostic information. Table 4.1 gives sample discussion prompts.

Prompts like these can be used in a verbal discussion with the whole class in the first session to elicit initial thoughts about the upcoming service-learning experience. While the responses are not reflections *per se*, the goal of the discussion is to

Table 4.1. Sample prompts to evaluate knowledge of service-learning and reflective practice

1. What do we mean by service-learning?
2. Who is doing the learning?
3. What might you learn?
4. What might you learn about teaching English learners in the community that you aren't learning here in the course or from your textbook?
5. How might you connect the service-learning experience to what you are learning in the TESOL program here?
6. In what way do you think your teaching – or the after-school program in general – will have an impact on the ELs?
7. How will you know if the learners' English is improving?
8. How much improvement do you think you will see in 4 weeks [8 sessions]?
9. To what extent might you learn about the education system or the facilities or resources that the ELs and their families have access to?
10. Besides working with learners on their English, what other contributions might you make?
11. How are you the same as or different from the children we will be working with?
12. What might you learn from the ELs themselves? What might they share with you? Do you think you will learn anything about what they are good at? Or about how they learn? Or about their language or experiences or the challenges they face?
13. In what way do you think our being there might have a negative impact?
14. How might you use what you learn in this experience in the future?
15. One of the ways you will be assessed is through reflection. What do you understand by reflection? How do you interpret critical reflection?
16. What aspects of the service-learning experience might you reflect on to demonstrate your learning in terms of your academic/cognitive, professional, social/civic development, and personal growth?

plant seeds to get preservice teachers to start thinking and reflecting in an intentional and targeted way. If time is too limited for such a class discussion, the prompts could be modified to form a survey for completion by individuals outside of class.

> **Points for Reflection**
> - In view of your understanding of service-learning and its goals, can you give reasons why these question prompts are suggested in Table 4.1? For example, what is the significance of asking questions 4, 10, 11?
> - Would you use similar prompts with your preservice teachers?
> - What might you ask your preservice teachers that is different?
> - How would you follow up on responses to these prompts?
> - What would you do with the information revealed in the responses?

Even at this initial stage, there is potential for reflective thinking. Follow-up prompts push preservice ESOL teachers to build on their responses so they will get used to clearly and fully explaining their thinking and justifying their claims. When they have a chance to elaborate on, justify, or revise their responses, it can help deepen their thinking.

Strategies for follow-up can include:

- paraphrasing responses to check for understanding
- keeping silent to prompt preservice teachers to revise or expand their responses
- asking how or why questions
- explicitly asking preservice teachers to clarify or expand on or justify their responses.

Instructors should try to ask follow-up questions in a natural and nurturing way to motivate participation and demonstrate that they are not simply running through a checklist of questions. Feedback, like "not quite" or "good" or even "ok", should be limited because thinking should not be evaluated at this stage. That said, non-verbal responses, like "mmhmm" or a nod or smile can encourage speakers to continue. To see an example of what this full discussion might look like, and what we can learn from it, see Table 5.1 in Chapter 5 (p. 121).

Discussing the meaning and purpose of service-learning as a class should include thinking about community needs (reflection standard indicator 3, NYLC, 2008) and the important roles that the preservice ESOL teachers have and those that the community partners have in addressing the needs. It is also crucial to make sure the preservice ESOL teachers understand the reciprocal nature of the relationship so that perceptions of a "savior complex" are not conveyed. In other words, the preservice teachers need to realize that they are not there to "save" the ELs; rather, they need to think about an asset-based approach and understand that everyone contributes to the experience, and everyone benefits through interaction and sharing information, knowledge, and skills, resulting in a stronger community. Instructors might consider assigning small groups to outline the roles and contributions of preservice teachers and community participants and identify ways that all benefit from the service-learning experience. Small group dialogue allows peers to get to know each other better and build a community of learners, which helps build rapport and trust. This is important for creating a safe space to share thoughts, find and give support, and for giving and receiving feedback on reflections.

Finally, preservice teachers should know that there is an expectation that they will work hard and display professionalism at the service-learning site. They should be aware of the challenges they will face, the lack of easy solutions to problems, and the possibility that they may feel pushed outside of their comfort zone at times. Instructors should reassure them that they are not alone, their concerns will be heard, and they will have access to support throughout the service-learning experience. Opportunities to discuss with partners any anxieties or stress they have about the service-learning experience can be helpful. Their thoughts here, though informal, may be considered as pre-reflections in anticipation of the service-learning experience.

PREPARE PRESERVICE ESOL TEACHERS FOR REFLECTION IN TESOL SERVICE-LEARNING

As explained in Chapter 2 and required by indicator 3 of the service-learning reflection standard (NYLC, 2008), effective reflection requires open-mindedness and high-level cognitive skills. Beyond simply describing and explaining, individuals need to be observant, perceptive, self-aware, analytical, and they need to think critically, develop metacognition, problem-solving skills, and a willingness to challenge existing assumptions, beliefs, and norms. Often reflections are superficial or reveal "reinforced stereotypes, interpretation based on unchallenged assumptions, inappropriate generalizations on the basis of limited data, shallow analysis that yields simplistic solutions to complex issues" (Ash et al., 2005, p. 52). It is essential, therefore, for instructors to prepare preservice ESOL teachers to reflect, structure reflections to scaffold development, and provide feedback.

The first and second reflection standard indicators for service-learning (NYLC, 2008) necessitate a variety of reflection activities before, during, and after the service-learning experience. While not all reflection activities will be assessed, some will, so preservice ESOL teachers need to understand what is expected of them; we cannot assume that they all know what reflection is in this context. The initial targeted discussion or survey responses should provide instructors with some insight but, as Hickson (2020) points out, individuals are likely at different stages of understanding and readiness to reflect. For this reason, it is important to share clear expectations and provide opportunities for preservice teachers to practice applying their understanding in advance.

It helps to outline the benefits of reflective practice with preservice teachers, most important of which is that effective reflection enhances learning. They need to be aware that reflection is more than a description of the service-learning experience. It is a process that involves: observing, interpreting, examining, searching for root causes, becoming aware of personal perspective and biases, considering multiple perspectives and influences, discussing with others, asking questions, challenging beliefs and norms, evaluating findings and forming possible conclusions, and suggesting implications for future actions. As such, reflection is not a quick task for the purpose of solving problems, nor is it an academic exercise. Preservice teachers should be forewarned that improving their reflective practice has many benefits but it does not mean that problems will be prevented or solved (Averett & Arnd-Caddigan, 2014). Rather, as Rogers (2002) explains, reflection is a way for us to make our experiences meaningful.

To illustrate the steps in the reflective process with a simple example, preservice teachers might reflect on a familiar experience, such as what they had for breakfast. Maybe some only had time to grab a coffee on the way to class and this can be examined further. Table 4.2 shows possible points that might arise throughout the reflection process.

If there is any confusion or frustration with this activity, preservice teachers should be reassured that the reflective process will become clearer with practice. Also, the process is not necessarily linear, as thinking returns to the observation throughout, and may return to other stages before moving towards a conclusion. In addition, the process can take some time, so most reflections (like those in regular journal entries) do not involve all of the stages of the process at one time and conclusions may not be reached until later. In fact, some findings may be inconclusive, which suggests that more investigation may be needed, or that multiple contributing factors may be in play, which could be an acceptable conclusion. The important point is that the process of reflecting leads to new meanings and understandings. In other words, reflecting in a meaningful way can lead to learning.

To remind preservice ESOL teachers of the professional skills they can reflect on in service-learning, it may be useful to have them complete a survey of their perceived competency levels before the service-learning experience. For an example, see Table 4.3, which is based on the self-assessment survey in the *European portfolio for student teachers of languages* (Newby et al., 2007) and draws on the Sheltered Instruction Observation Protocol (SIOP) (Echevarría et al., 2017) and the TESOL standards (www.tesol.org/teacher-prep-standards).

Table 4.2. Example reflection process: breakfast

Observe and describe event	Only had coffee for breakfast
Interpret event	Intentional vs unintentional action? Norm vs unusual? Etc. How did it make you feel? Did it affect others?
Examine event	How much time was there for breakfast? Was this the preferred breakfast?
Search for root causes	Lack of time/got up late/felt sleepy/needed caffeine/not hungry/on a diet/no food in the house/no money for food…
Be aware of self	Not a morning person/can't eat immediately
Ask questions	Is this a habit or a one-off? Is coffee required? Why? Is food needed for breakfast? What are the physical effects with just coffee for breakfast?
Seek other perspectives/influences	Poor time management/lack of concern for health/scheduling of classes isn't convenient
Discuss with others	Is this common with other people? If so, what are the reasons? Are there common issues that affect breakfast choices, e.g. scheduling of classes? How does coffee vs food for breakfast affect other people?
Challenge beliefs and norms	Who says coffee for breakfast is bad? Who says breakfast is necessary? Why do classes have to start so early? Is attending classes necessary?
Suggest conclusions	Maybe more than coffee is needed. Maybe some people learn best by attending classes
Consider implications and future action	Set an earlier alarm/stock kitchen with granola bars, fruit/get a job for money/advocate for a later class time

The purpose of using a survey is not to reduce reflections to a checklist, or as an evaluation of learning, but rather to help individuals narrow their thinking to specific language teaching competencies and develop self-awareness. The results can provide useful information to reflect on as the experience progresses. Completing the survey again after the service-learning experience can help preservice teachers identify changes for their final reflection assignment. I suggest assigning this as an ungraded task or counting its completion towards a participation grade.

Points for Reflection
- Would you use pre and post surveys in your context to promote reflection?
- How might you adapt the survey in Table 4.3 to meet your needs?

Table 4.3. Sample survey of TESOL competencies (1 is strongly disagree; 5 is strongly agree)

Lesson design	1	2	3	4	5
1. I can design language activities that will motivate learning and engage ELs.					
2. I can plan appropriate lesson stages, e.g. building background, presentation of new content, guided practice, application, consolidation.					
3. I can plan differentiated instruction for diverse learners.					

Lesson delivery	1	2	3	4	5
4. I can help ELs activate their schema and make connections to new information.					
5. I can provide comprehensible input and instructions.					
6. I can use strategies that help ELs notice language features.					
7. I can use different techniques to scaffold language learning.					
8. I can use a range of question types effectively.					
9. I can manage the lesson stages in a timely manner with logical transitions from one stage to another.					
10. I can demonstrate cultural sensitivity and encourage ELs to value cultural and linguistic diversity.					

Assessing learners	1	2	3	4	5
11. I can use various techniques to monitor and assess ELs' comprehension and language performance.					
12. I can identify strengths and areas for improvement in an EL's language performance.					
13. I can assess an EL's language skills according to target criteria.					
14. I can analyze language learners' errors and identify reasons why they may have occurred.					
15. I can use assessment results to inform my teaching and plan language lessons for individuals and groups.					

CRITICAL REFLECTION IN SERVICE-LEARNING

Indicator 5 of the reflection standard for service-learning requires participants to examine a variety of social and civic issues (NYLC, 2008). This standard is embedded in my approach to reflective practice in service-learning, which includes a social justice perspective and critical reflection; but this can be challenging for pre-service teachers and guidance is needed, as Eyler (2002a) points out: "[s]tudents … are more likely to develop the capacity for critical thought if they are challenged both by surprising experiences and by reflective teachers who help them explore these experiences and question their fundamental assumptions about their world"

(p. 521). In my TESOL courses, therefore, we spend time discussing what it means to reflect critically. With critical reflection, the search for understanding requires that preservice teachers analyze interactions and behaviors with awareness about their own identity, beliefs, and values. I encourage them to search beyond initial assumptions for root causes of events they observe during service-learning. I also encourage them to think about issues of diversity, equity, and inclusion that are so relevant in multilingual contexts. Where it is appropriate, TESOL instructors can facilitate discussions to prepare preservice teachers to engage in this kind of thinking and reflection prompts can be designed to compel preservice teachers to ask hard questions about the norms they operate under and "challenge policies, laws, and social institutions in the context of their experiences and readings, discussions, and written assignments"' (Jacoby, 2014, p. 43). See Chapter 2 for more on critical reflection.

A SOCIAL JUSTICE PERSPECTIVE

For instructors who decide to take a social justice perspective to service-learning reflection, there are certain steps they might take to make the concept of social justice less abstract. This is important as Pipe and Stephens (2021) point out:

> When discussing challenging topics about identity, power structures, oppression, etc., students need scholarly starting points. Additionally, if critical arguments of self are pushed too soon without this scholarly foundation, learners may quickly foreclose on any discussion in a fight-or-flight response resulting from being pushed beyond their growth zone. (p. 130)

First, it is useful to have a conversation about why there is a need for service-learning and what social justice means. The importance of conversation or discussion cannot be stressed enough, as Palpacuer Lee et al. (2018) assert: "social interaction and systematic reflection that are fundamental to CBSL [community-based service-learning] lead students to deconstruct their cultural assumptions and stereotypes and to (re)negotiate their identities and positionalities in relation to the communities in which they live and work" (p. 177). So, together, preservice teachers could brainstorm a list of injustices that might affect ELs specifically and immigrants generally. For example, issues might include a lack of qualified ESOL teachers, the limited availability of ESOL programs and other language programs, support services, and resources, the marginalization of multilingual learners, lack of awareness of ELs' legal rights. The issue of linguistic imperialism may arise and instructors should acknowledge that this is a valid concern, yet as ESOL teachers, our job should be to help ELs expand their linguistic repertoire to include English, not replace their first language with English. Nieto (2018) suggests asking critical questions, like "which classes meet in the basement?" (p. 157), or who has access to prestigious courses or opportunities that open doors for students? Who has access to sports and clubs and transportation? Who has support at home, such as books, computers, internet access, adequate nutrition? Do government/education/institution policies help or harm ELs (reflection standard indicator 5, NYLC, 2008)? In the wider community, issues might include forms of discrimination in terms of access to jobs, housing, medical care, voting rights, services in their language, and so on. Once critical questions are raised, preservice teachers can start thinking about possible ways to start addressing needs.

Ideally, there would be time to build a scholarly foundation in social justice through readings and activities on beliefs, values, and identity, community problems and needs, culturally responsive pedagogy, and civic responsibility. Sections from relevant books can be assigned reading or used in class lectures or activities. For example, if time allows, a jigsaw reading activity could be conducted where expert groups read and discuss different sections of a text. Instructors may ask for a summary of the text or provide questions to prompt reflective thinking.

Points for Reflection

- What books or resources do you know of that might be useful for explaining the concept of social justice or culturally responsive teaching?
- How might you use such books in your context?
- What prompts might you use to help preservice ESOL teachers reflect on texts they read?
- What activities might be effective in your context for raising awareness of social justice issues?

If, after discussing social issues, some preservice teachers feel a sense of powerlessness in terms of effecting positive change, support should be provided. They should be reassured that raising issues and starting conversations is a good first step. While it is not realistic to think that one service-learning experience will solve problems, it is an opportunity to think about future actions that can contribute to a more just world.

If time is limited, preservice teachers might reflect on selected quotes, definitions, or pertinent excerpts from various sources. They can share interpretations and identify the ideas that are most meaningful to them or discuss what they think is the most valuable point. The experience of reading, interpreting, questioning, and interacting are part of the reflective process and the content helps explain the concept of social justice.

Alternatively, specific prompts can be provided for oral and/or written reflection, such as:

- Why do you think some people stereotype non-English speakers and what are the consequences?
- Why do you think some people do not want immigrants in their community?
- What can be done to help persuade people that immigrants can add value to a community?

IDENTITY AND VALUES ACTIVITIES

It should be acknowledged that simply having conversations about inequities, power, privilege, and oppression, especially with predominantly white, middle-class, English-speaking preservice teachers does not guarantee that they will be prepared to respond to issues in practice (Pirbhai-Illich, 2013). Nor does it mean they will reflect on them meaningfully. It can, however, start to raise their awareness of how their identities, values, beliefs, and assumptions provide the lens through which they see themselves and others, which shapes how they reflect on the service-learning experience. For example, those with fairly privileged backgrounds may hold deficit-oriented views about the capacities of ELs (Becker & Paul, 2015), or they may think that the way they were taught or developed is the preferred way for everyone. In other words, "a norm developed by the white middle class is universalised as 'the' norm for all groups, no matter what their cultural background" (Pirbhai-Illich, 2013, p. 82).

Instructors can help raise preservice teachers' self-awareness for critical reflection because being aware of their identities, beliefs, values, and assumptions, as well as the intersectionality of their identities, can lead to greater understanding about their roles and the dynamics of interactions with others. This aligns with NYLC (2008) service-learning reflection standard indicator 4, which requires that participants "examine their preconceptions and assumptions in order to explore and understand their roles and responsibilities as citizens" (reflection section). This focus on the self can be difficult for preservice teachers, especially if they think their beliefs are being judged. It can also seem contradictory when, in some academic contexts, we are taught to be objective and "remove ourselves" from the work. Many journals, for example, even in the field of language education, do not publish papers with the personal pronoun "I", yet for reflective practice, the self is central.

Various resources and activities can be used to raise greater awareness of self-identity and knowledge of social inequities, such as: attitude or belief surveys (Ruiz-Ordonez, et al. 2020; Wilhelm et al., 2001), creating identity charts or identity visuals (see https://www.facinghistory.org/resource-library/teaching-strategies/identity-charts or Busch, 2010), relevant stories, videos, or podcasts to prompt discussion about identity, beliefs, values, and assumptions, journal writing with specific prompts about identity, like: *How might others describe you?, How do your perceptions of yourself and other peoples' perceptions of you affect your interactions with others?*, and activities on civic identity (Gottlieb & Robinson, 2006).

Care should be taken, however, in selecting and implementing activities because the point is to reflect on identity and norms and raise awareness of social injustices, not to create divides or feelings of anxiety. Bolger (2018) explains, for example, that the effectiveness of "privilege walk" activities depends on the participation of non-privileged groups, and, while the message may be powerful, there is a cost in terms of exposing vulnerabilities, causing fear of being judged, or creating feelings of destructive guilt. As an alternative, she offers a "privilege for sale" activity (https://www.socialjusticetoolbox.com/activity/privilege-for-sale/).

The choice of activities will depend on the specific context and course goals. Instructors need to create a safe, non-judgmental environment for activities and discussions to ensure that preservice teachers understand how self-awareness will help them reflect in meaningful ways. Activities should be implemented in conjunction with guided discussion to avoid creating divides or further entrenching deficit-oriented views and stereotypes of ELs and their learning capacities. Additional support and resources for individuals should be available if there is a need.

> **Points for Reflection**
> - In your context, how important is it to take a social justice approach to critical reflection?
> - What activities might you use to help raise awareness of identity and social justice issues (if appropriate)?

ENGAGE PRESERVICE ESOL TEACHERS IN REFLECTION BEFORE SERVICE-LEARNING

When service-learning and related concepts (such as self-awareness, identity, civic responsibility, social justice, reflection, critical reflection) have been discussed and expectations for reflection assignments have been shared, a reflection task prior to the service experience can be assigned to give preservice ESOL teachers an opportunity to explore thoughts and questions about the upcoming service experience.

This provides the instructor with information to monitor understanding and social emotional connections. Eyler (2002a) makes the point that:

> it is common for students who participate in tutoring programs to have a number of stereotypes about the children they will work with and their families. Surfacing these preconceptions may help students be more observant ... Surfacing assumptions before the service experience can also expose students to the conflicts among their peers and among experts about ill-structured problems. (p. 524)

It may be useful to discuss assumptions, expectations, uncertainties and anxieties about the experience in groups before writing individual reflections. Preservice ESOL teachers could write their own reflection in a non-prescribed way that is meaningful to them, or, to increase chances that assumptions and other important issues emerge, targeted prompts could be provided, for example:

- How do you feel about participating in community service-learning?
- Why do you think these ELs need support through service-learning?
- How might your life experience be the same or different from the ELs?
- In what ways do you hope to make a contribution?
- What goals do you have for this service-learning experience?
- What do you think you will teach the ELs?
- What do you think the ELs will teach you?
- What do you think you will learn from the EL teachers in the school? from this service-learning experience in general?
- What questions/concerns/anxieties do you have about the service-learning experience?
- What kind of impact do you think the service-learning experience will have on your academic/cognitive development? professional growth? social/civic development? personal growth?
- What kind of impact do you think this service-learning experience will have on your sense of civic responsibility? on your future?

Thinking about the service-learning experience in advance and discussing thoughts and feelings with others can alleviate uncertainties and anxieties. Subsequently, reflections could be written as journal entries or short response essays.

Another reflection task at this early stage might be to write an expectations and goals statement. This could be based on the TESOL competencies survey (see Table 4.3) or other professional goals. Or it could focus on personal goals or civic identity or multiple goal areas.

Prior to the service experience, another reflection task that Eyler (2002a) suggests (and calls a "preflection" task) is to have participants write a letter to themselves about their expectations and learning goals and then open it at the end of the experience to determine the extent to which the goals were attained. The proviso here would be that goals could change or be modified during the experience in response to needs in the community. Such a letter could also be written to, or shared with, peers.

> **Points for Reflection**
> - What kind of "preflection" task might work in your TESOL service-learning context?
> - How similar or different would the prompts you use for "preflection" be to those listed above?
> - Would you assess "preflection" tasks?

Preparing preservice ESOL teachers for reflection in service-learning involves building understanding of various concepts, like self-awareness and social justice, as well as making expectations for reflection clear. It also means demonstrating that critical reflection is not an academic exercise, but a personal process for their learning which will be different for everyone. It can help shape beliefs and values, deepen understanding of self and interactions with others, and give insight into social issues. Preservice teachers need to be prepared for self-examination and, benefits aside, they need to be prepared for discomfort, and possible feelings of uncertainty, frustration, guilt, and anxiety.

ENGAGE PRESERVICE ESOL TEACHERS IN CRITICAL REFLECTION DURING SERVICE-LEARNING

The obvious difference in reflections *during* service-learning compared to *prior* to service-learning is that specific events (interactions, incidents, behaviors) are experienced during service-learning and thus can be identified and analyzed as the focus for reflection.

Some preservice ESOL teachers have trouble identifying relevant events, interactions, behaviors, or incidents to reflect on. To help them become observant and curious, I encourage preservice teachers to notice both positive and negative events, small or large. Even silence can be an observed event when it is unexpected because it begs the question, *why?* One activity that can help is peer observation. Rather than having everyone involved in EL teaching during each site visit during our service-learning experience, I assign some preservice teachers to observe their peers teaching. The observation tool they use is the Sheltered Instruction Observation Protocol (SIOP) (Echevarría et al., 2017), which focuses on eight components of a lesson. Though it is not necessary for one lesson to include everything on the protocol, the tool helps preservice teachers focus on manageable chunks, which helps them to isolate events. The SIOP protocol tool provides a checklist (Echevarría et al., 2017, pp. 309–311), on which I encourage preservice teachers to add specific details about events they observe. They can then refer to their SIOP checklist to select events to reflect on. Farrell (2019) cautions: "the danger is that RP [reflective practice] has now become too ritualized ... reduced to a set of prescriptive techniques for teachers to follow blindly" (pp. 59–60). I emphasize, therefore, that the SIOP checklist is simply a tool to inspire further reflection. I reiterate that SIOP and the other tools and strategies in this chapter are suggestions only, not prescriptions, and I encourage instructors to customize any tools and strategies to their specific context.

REFLECTION TYPES AND ARTIFACTS

Reflections before, during, and after service-learning experience can consist of many types and artifacts. We have already talked about the importance of dialogue, which can include sharing sessions or discussions during service-learning, involving:

- Pairs or groups or whole class
- Face-to-face or electronic (see Chapter 6 for the impacts of technology on reflective practice)
- Short, informal sharing of thoughts, such as "turn and talk" dialogues
- Detailed group analysis of events/forums
- Formal debriefings after each site visit.

Reflection artifacts can be produced both in class and outside of class and can include:

- Reflection journals/blogs/vlogs
- Statement of goals
- Quick writes and exit slips
- Collaborative reflections on Google Docs to make thinking visible
- Formal reflection papers
- Peer feedback forms
- Self-analysis reports
- Letters to self or others
- Multimodal reflections

- Audio and video recordings
- Presentations
- Role plays
- Debates
- Portfolios
- Artwork: paintings, posters, murals, sculptures
- Creative performances, skits, poetry, songs.

In this section, some of these artifacts will be highlighted with sample prompts to facilitate relevant reflections.

Recalling Eyler et al.'s (1996) four Cs for characterizing reflection: *continuous, connected, challenging,* and *contextualized,* there should be multiple cycles of reflection and feedback throughout the service-learning experience to monitor progress and help participants build metacognition and reflection skills. Reflection prompts should be crafted in a way that they are challenging and encourage connections between TESOL coursework, service experiences (events, observations, interactions), and broader issues. Prompts should also target desired learning points and development goals. This is not to say that informal and less guided reflection is not important. Indeed, quick writes (quick written responses to prompts at the end of session), oral debriefings, and pair and group dialogue provide opportunities for individuals to express feelings, share uncertainties, support, and encouragement with others. The point is that multiple opportunities to reflect in various ways are advised.

Points for Reflection
- What reflection types and artifacts do/would you use to facilitate reflective practice *during* service-learning?

FRAMEWORKS TO GUIDE REFLECTION

My experience supports research (Leeuwen et al., 2017; Schön, 1987) that shows that, without guidance, reflections can be superficial and uncritical. When I would ask preservice teachers to reflect on an experience without giving them any guidance, they would often struggle to find meaningful events to comment on, or they would simply describe what happened, or describe their feelings. In order to encourage greater focus and meaning, I have found it helpful to share a reflection framework with participants. Frameworks can be customized to align with the context of use and shared with preservice teachers to help guide their thinking.

Expanding the DEAL model (Ash & Clayton, 2009), for example, to help participants reflect on their TESOL service-learning experiences might look like this (italicized parts in original):

1. *Describe* experiences objectively with pertinent details. What events/interactions/actions/incidents were noticeable to you? Consider, for example, observations of English language learning that you saw and instances where learning did not occur.

2. *Examine* or analyze experiences in view of the learning objectives. Explore possible root causes for interactions/actions/incidents. Consider the resulting responses and possible alternative responses. Draw on language learning theory. Demonstrate curiosity, metacognition, critical reflection.

3. *Articulate your learning* and how it will impact your future practice and goals. Ask yourself: What did I learn? What did this event/interaction teach me? about ELs? about myself? about English language teaching and learning? about the education system? about the school? about community engagement? about power?
   - *How, specifically, did I learn it?* Is there evidence of EL learning? Did peers influence me? Did TESOL coursework have an impact? Is there a connection to language learning theory?
   - *Why does this learning matter? or why is it significant?* Why did I notice this? Is this an anomaly or a pattern? Might this event/interaction occur in other contexts with other individuals?
   - *In what ways will I use this learning? or what goals shall I set in accordance with what I have learned in order to improve myself, the quality of my learning, or the quality of my future experiences or service?* Will this awareness affect the way I interact with ELs/colleagues/community partners in the future? Has this experience helped me to improve my ESOL teaching competencies? Has my thinking or my beliefs about ELs/the education system changed? Has this experience helped confirm that I am on an appropriate career path? Will I engage in community service in the future?

Another framework I have used is Jacoby's (2014) *What? So what? Now what? framework,* which is particularly useful for short service-learning projects.

1. *What?* refers to what happened, what was observed, what the resulting feelings were.

2. *So what?* refers to what was learned from it, evolving understandings, new connections to prior knowledge, theory, and coursework, and why the learning is important.

3. *Now what?* refers to resulting actions, ways it might change future actions.

Like DEAL, Jacoby's (2014) framework focuses on learning and on how the experience may impact future action or goals, which are key elements in service-learning. The question prompts encourage participants to target thinking about specific events or observations and they can require increasingly complex thinking. Hullender (2015) makes the point that "[r]eflective questions that encourage students to move from lower cognitive ways of thinking to questions that encourage students to explore a more critical analysis of a situation, often by acknowledging various perspectives and positions, increase the likelihood that a more transformative experience might occur" (p. 76). Specific question prompts can be added to focus responses on the target context.

> **Points for Reflection**
> - In your view, for reflections to be effective for learning, should a framework be applied?
> - Consider the DEAL model (Ash & Clayton, 2009) and Jacoby's (2014) reflection framework. Would either be useful for facilitating reflections in your TESOL service-learning context?
> - In your context, would you facilitate reflection by providing specific prompts or would you suggest that preservice teachers reflect in a way that is meaningful to them? Think about the reasons for your choice.

Regardless of which reflection framework or model is selected, simply sharing it with preservice teachers is probably not enough. Instructors should also demonstrate how to apply the chosen reflective framework through a "think aloud", or by co-constructing a reflection as a class, or by analyzing a model reflection (see Table 4.4).

SHARING REFLECTION SAMPLES OR MODELS

Besides sharing frameworks for reflection, samples or models of reflections can be shared to provide guidance on the expected end product. Samples or models illustrate expectations for preservice teachers who don't think in the abstract or who have difficulty visualizing a finished product. "Students learn more deeply when they have multiple concrete referents for abstract concepts" (Eyler, 2002a, p. 521).

When I was a beginning teacher, I was hesitant to provide models to my students because I thought they would be tempted to copy. I have since learned that it is possible to use models to guide students in creating their own original pieces of work. It is often helpful to analyze each move in the model to show its purpose (as in Table 4.4). Ideally, models should be authentic and taken from TESOL service-learning

Table 4.4. Analysis of a sample reflection

Sample TESOL service-learning reflection excerpt	Analysis of moves Applying the What? So what? Now what? framework (Jacoby, 2014)
(1) I worked one-on-one with a student who was a very beginning level English speaker … (2) if he was asked only in English to do even the littlest task, he would get upset and try to leave the room. However, if he was asked to do the exact same thing in Spanish, he was more than willing to do it. I would write sentences first in his L1, he would copy it, and then I would translate the sentence into English and he would copy that as well. Then we would practice reading the English aloud together, by having him repeat small chunks of the language at a time	(1) provides some background details (2) describes the observed event = problem and how it was handled. This answers the What? question
Through this experience, (3) I learned the importance of an individual's first language. While the idea behind teaching a second language is to use the L2 as much as possible, there are times when you just cannot …	(3) states specific learning point = importance of L1. This answers the So what? question
I think that (4) we live in a culture where we want to squash the L1 and have them only speaking in the L2 … However, (5) this not only destroys that culture that is associated with the L1 and that individual, it also is impractical and nearly impossible – the L1 is extremely important …	(4) identifies injustice here = social pressure to use L2 (5) explains consequences
(6) This experience has taught me that the L1 is acceptable to use, especially when the student knows the concept without having the proper vocabulary in the L2. Then this moment can become a teachable moment where the vocabulary that the student is looking for can be taught and then acquire, instead of being thrown out because the meaning is not there …	(6) elaborates on learning point
(7) I feel as though I learned how to be adaptable while teaching. There were things that did not always go according to plan and I had to think on my feet to adapt to the needs of the ELs in the moment. (8) This is something I do not have much experience with, but definitely will continue to work on	(7) identifies related learning point = need to be adaptable (8) sets goal for future EL teaching = thinking on feet and being adaptable. This answers the Now what? question

experiences or other service-learning contexts. When reflecting on service-learning, the individual and personal nature of the experience means that copying is unlikely, but if, for some reason, it does occur, feedback can be given along with strategies on how to avoid it. This can mean simply and explicitly warning preservice teachers about plagiarism, or comparing the plagiarized reflection side-by-side with the sample reflection.

Identifying the moves in this way shows how reflection frameworks can be applied. It also demonstrates the effectiveness of including specific details and shows how each statement has a specific function. If some preservice teachers need further scaffolding, sentence frames could be pulled from such a model, for example:

- An example of EL learning that I noticed was ...
- A missed opportunity was ...
- We are working in a culture where ...
- If this happens again, I will ...
- I will continue to work on ...

Sharing samples or models of both effective and less effective reflections can make the differences more explicit for participants.

COMMON ARTIFACTS

Now let's look a little more closely at some of the more common artifacts used for reflection, such as dialogues/discussions, written journals, e-journals/audio recordings/blogs/vlogs, reflection papers or reports, roleplays with reflection discussion, and presentations. It is advised to reflect frequently and use different artifacts. Indeed, a choice of artifact might be given in some contexts.

Dialogue and Discussions

Dialogue and discussion is an essential step in reflective practice that should be frequently organized to foster reflection. Let us recall one of Rogers's (2002) criteria for reflection: "Reflection needs to happen in community, in interaction with others" (p. 845). She explains that discussing experiences with others has multiple benefits. First, articulating thoughts compels participants to clearly organize their thinking for others, which can expose incoherence, omissions, or misunderstandings. Second, feedback can be shared, which can affirm some ideas and constructively critique others. It can also result in the recovery of details that may have been dismissed by someone when thinking alone. Third, it allows different perspectives and new understandings to be shared, which helps transform thinking. As such, dialogue provides support for the process of inquiry by inspiring new questions and curiosities.

Oral interactions can be short, informal dialogue sessions to brainstorm ideas prior to written reflections. One way to facilitate this is to have preservice teachers write on post-it notes their thoughts about what is going well and what is not going well. As a class, they can share the thoughts and identify emerging themes to categorize them. This can lead to further discussion and reflection. The anonymous post-it notes can help reticent individuals share their thinking, and the grouping of thoughts can affirm shared ideas, as well as reveal ideas that others may not have thought of. Sharing perspectives in this and other reflection tasks can also help improve reflection skills.

More intentional, targeted discussions can be implemented in order to build reflection skills. For this, guiding frameworks and prompts can be used as scaffolding. Some instructors may require written notes or summaries of the discussion. The use of collaborative writing platforms, like GoogleDocs, is very useful for this as another way to make thinking visible as instructors and peers can view responses to prompts and ideas as they are written down in real time. Ideally, discussion can be done in person or synchronously online, but electronic discussion boards can also be used. See Chapter 5 for a discussion of the impacts of technology on reflective practice.

Reflection Journal

Reflection journals, whether electronic or traditional, are a very useful tool for helping preservice teachers reflect continuously (daily/weekly). Journal reflections can be written at home so they don't take up valuable class time or community engagement time. Instructors should provide guidance on this so that individuals don't treat it simply as a log for describing service-learning activities rather than a space for analysis and reflection (Bringle & Hatcher, 1999). To this end, the purpose of the reflection journal and how it should be organized needs to be established in advance. Bringle and Hatcher (1999, p. 182) suggest that instructors could choose a specific type of reflective journal for participants to use. They provide four examples:

1. *Key Phrase Journal* – a description and discussion of service activities integrated with key terms, like scaffolding, noticing, inclusion, differentiation, social justice.
2. *Double Entry Journal* – a description of an event (such as evidence of EL learning) on one side and interpretations and reactions on the other.
3. *Critical Incident Journal* – identification of a key event with response. Prompt questions from the model frameworks above would work well here.

4. *Three-Part Journal* – includes (a) description of service experience or event, (b) analysis of how the service experience relates to course material, and (c) explanation of connections and impacts to personal values, beliefs, assumptions. Prompt questions from the model frameworks above would work well here.

Some instructors may set up a continuous journal in which preservice teachers respond to the same prompts after every session. Standardized prompts help preservice teachers build a habit of identifying and reflecting on events and interactions in terms of causes, effects, and impacts. Alternatively, specific prompts on targeted topics could be provided, such as:

- Reflect on how you dealt with language error correction in your service-learning experience and how effective it was. What factors impacted the effectiveness of your approach? Will you change anything next time?
- Reflect on the strategies you used to differentiate instruction when there were mixed levels of language proficiency. How effective were they? How do you know? What factors impacted the effectiveness of your strategies? Would you change anything next time?

Another approach would be to structure the reflection journal in a way that the prompts align directly with the service-learning development goals. A choice, in terms of which goals to focus on, could be given. The benefit of this kind of structure is that all the goals would be kept in the forefront of the preservice teachers' minds. Examples of prompts for each development goal are listed below.

Academic/cognitive development:

- What language learning theory did you draw on this week to try to solve a problem? How similar was it in practice to the explanations in your coursework?
- Did you seek and find the root cause of a problem that you observed this week? Explain.
- Did you notice any progress in your performance this week? Explain.

Professional development :

- What language teaching competencies have you been working on this week? What progress did you make? What teaching competencies do you need to continue to work on?
- In what ways did you scaffold language learning this week? How effective were they? How do you know? How will this impact your future practice?
- What happened this week to make you think that this context may/may not be a good fit for your future career?

Social/civic development:

- In what ways did you collaborate with others this week? How successful was the collaboration and why?
- What did you learn from an EL this week? From a peer?
- Did anything happen this week that made you think about possible future community engagement opportunities?

Personal development:

- Were any of your personal beliefs challenged this week?
- Did you surprise yourself in any way this week in the way you responded to someone or something? What does that tell you about yourself?
- Did you learn anything this week about how you are similar or different from the ELs?

Points for Reflection
- Do these prompts give you any ideas for other prompts you might use in your context?

Yet another approach for journals provides choices for the focus of reflection and choice of prompts to respond to. Table 4.5 presents an example of instructions that I use for such a reflection journal.

Regardless of the type of journal or prompts used, instructions for journals should be discussed with the class in advance to ensure that the expectations are clear. If time is limited for giving instructor feedback every week, journals can be shared with peers for feedback. The benefit of this is that ideas can be confirmed and/or challenged through a broader range of perspectives, and learning points can be shared amongst peers. Encouraging preservice teachers to revisit their reflections in the journal over time enables them to track development in their thinking and learning, builds their self-awareness and metacognition, and provides evidence they can use in final reflection assignments.

E-journals/audio recordings/blogs/vlogs

An alternative to a reflection journal, is an e-journal, reflection blog (weblog), or vlog (video log). Like journals, they can be a specific type, they should be guided by frameworks and prompts, and be completed regularly. But, unlike traditional journals, reflection e-journals, blogs, and vlogs have the advantage of integrating images, audio recordings, and other modalities of expression, rather than relying solely on print. Preservice teachers who prefer to reflect verbally can use this

Table 4.5. Sample instructions for a weekly reflection journal

---

Weekly reflection journal guidelines

Create a Google Doc and post weekly reflection entries in which you reflect on the service-learning experience. Be sure to share access with your TESOL professor and peers if desired. Your journal will be awarded full points for regular completion provided it meets expectations of timeliness and demonstrates thinking. Any comments I make will be formative, intended to help guide you towards your academic/cognitive, professional, social/civic, and personal development. Your reflection journal will become a useful source of data to revisit for your final reflection assignment.

Below are three focus areas and various prompts to guide your reflections. You can choose which focus area and which prompts you want to respond to in your reflection.

1. Identify a meaningful language learning event or interaction that occurred during the week. Why was it meaningful to you? How do you know if learning occurred or didn't occur? What worked or didn't work? What was the underlying reason? What have you learned from it? How might this event impact your future English language teaching?

2. Connect specific TESOL course content (e.g., a language learning theory or principle discussed in your TESOL program) to an event or interaction you observed or experienced this week. Evaluate the effectiveness of the content/theory/principle in practice. What have you learned from this? How might this affect your future teaching?

   Possible aspects to consider:

   - Teaching approaches: What TESOL methods/approaches/ techniques were used this week? How effective were they? How do you know? What evidence did you see of learning? How was instruction differentiated? How effective was that?

   - Language: Is there a range of L1s? What language strengths and needs were noticeable this week? What was the cause of some of the language challenges? (How) were they being addressed? How is L1 perceived by the ELs? By the community teacher? By your peers? By you?

   - Diversity, equity, inclusion: How diverse are the ELs? How are they the same as or different from you? Were attempts made to include ELs as individuals with linguistic and cultural capital this week? i.e. Do observed interactions suggest that the ELs are viewed with a deficit mindset or an asset mindset? What efforts were made to engage in culturally responsive teaching?

   - Social justice issues: What policies and practices impact how this program/school / system works? Who has power? Who doesn't? Were you aware of any injustices this week?

3. Identify an event you observed or experienced this week that connects to one of the goals you set for your service-learning experience in terms of your academic/cognitive, professional, social/civic, personal development. How is your goal linked to the event? What progress are you making? Why or why not? How will you overcome any challenges going forward?

---

alternative. In addition, reflection blogs and vlogs can be more creative and thus more attractive to viewers, and potentially garner more feedback if URLs are shared beyond the community of learners. The use of technology for reflections can promote digital literacy and creativity; however, some individuals prefer writing, and privacy issues for use of images and public consumption can be problematic. To address this, instructors could offer choices or alternate between traditional and digital reflections. Parameters can be set to limit viewer access and permissions for image use can be sought to avoid infringement. More on using technology in service-learning reflections is found in Chapter 6.

> **Points for Reflection**
> - What type of reflection journal would you assign in a TESOL service-learning context?

Reflection Paper or Report

Some students (and instructors) prefer the traditional mode of writing a reflection paper (essay) or report. During the service-learning, this may involve a choice of targeted prompts for which the paper provides a response, or the paper may focus on specific incidents and align with a selected reflection framework, such as DEAL (Ash & Clayton, 2009).

Role Play with Reflection Discussion

Having preservice teachers perform a role play of critical incidents from the service-learning experience can be useful in contexts where peers have not been present for the same experience or incident. It can be more motivating to express an incident through a role play than through verbal or written description for both the presenters and the viewers, as it brings the incident to life, making it more immediate and engaging. Importantly, the role play is followed by discussion which allows different interpretations and perspectives to be shared. This can be very helpful, especially when challenging issues arise that would benefit from eliciting multiple suggestions of ways to address them.

Presentation

A live or recorded presentation can be an effective alternative to a written reflection. Presentations can be individual or collaborative and allow presenters to integrate visuals and other modes of communication, making them creative and often motivating. Specific guidelines can be provided to limit the amount of freedom presenters have in terms of content. Depending on the focus of the presentation, it can be followed by discussion with viewers. Like the role play, a presentation can mean a wider audience is involved so different perspectives can be shared and feedback given. This is particularly important during service-learning because there is still time for individuals to address any issues in their service as well as improve their skills in reflection.

Regardless of the artifact chosen for reflection, facilitating reflection during service-learning involves providing frequent opportunities for reflection of various types, scaffolded with relevant frameworks and guiding prompts, and, importantly, followed up with feedback. Many of the same types and artifacts can be used for reflection after the service-learning experience, though the focus at the end is generally more comprehensive and summative. We turn to this next.

ENGAGE PRESERVICE ESOL TEACHERS IN REFLECTION AFTER SERVICE-LEARNING

At the completion of the service project, reflection typically involves some sort of consolidation of learning. It is important to reiterate that the final reflection should not be the only reflection of the service-learning experience. At this stage of reflection, there is an opportunity for preservice teachers to debrief and engage in dialogue, where they can express how/if the service-learning experience shaped their consciousness, that is, ways they now view the world that they were unaware of before and which will influence how they view the world going forward. Also, at this point preservice teachers can revisit academic content to view it through "new eyes" and with new understandings. It is this stage of reflection that has the potential to lead to transformative learning.

Often post-experience reflections are shared with peers and community participants and beyond. Usually they are assessed, but they don't have to be. Artifacts employed after service-learning might include those used during service-learning as well as:

- Post-service-learning experience surveys
- Final reflection papers
- Presentations
- Response to letters to self or others
- Portfolios
- Artwork: paintings, posters, murals, sculptures
- Creative performances: songs, skits, poetry
- Multimodal reflections
- Story telling/narrative inquiry (see Foste, 2018)
- Thank you letters to community partner
- Publications, conference presentations.

A comparison of journal reflections from pre, during, and post experience can be extremely useful in determining progress. Preservice teachers can also complete a post-experience survey and compare results to those from a pre-experience survey (see Table 4.3 above). They can also revisit other artifacts used, such as goal statements, letters to self. Highlighting initial statements in "preflections" or early reflections about beliefs, uncertainties, frustrations, challenges, problems, and aligning them with later statements about changed beliefs, increased confidence, resolutions to problems, new approaches, and so on enables preservice teachers to audit their own learning and pinpoint evidence of changes in academic/cognitive, professional, social and civic, or personal skills and dispositions. That said, we cannot expect that all changes that are identified will denote improvement; nor can we expect that one semester-long (or shorter) service-learning project will be enough to result in transformative learning. This is particularly true in reference to critical reflection in which social justice issues are explored. However, it is hoped that the process of reflection on service-learning will at least lead to development in some or all of the goal areas and to other benefits of reflective practice, like strengthening communities.

Prompts employed after service-learning may be similar to those used during service-learning, but some would be more focused on overall progress in the service-learning project. Sample prompts at the final stage might be:

- What is the most important lesson you have learned from your service-learning experience? How will you use what you learned going forward?
- What future goals do you have as a result of this service-learning experience?
- What did you learn about working with diverse populations that you didn't know before?
- Looking back at your "preflection", how were your beliefs or assumptions about the service-learning experience and about working with ELs confirmed or changed?
- Did you learn anything in this service-learning experience that will help you to advocate for ELs in the future? Explain.
- What did you learn about yourself through this service-learning experience?
- Do you think the service-learning project helped to address the community needs? Why or why not?

For instructors who encourage a social justice perspective, prompts might include:

- What social issues (inequities, injustices) were you made aware of during this service-learning experience?
- How equitable is education for ELs in the community?
- What further research can be done to better understand the social issues?

- How do community members, academic institutions, stakeholders, politicians, etc. perceive the issues/ELs?
- In addition to raising awareness of the issues and needs, what other steps might be taken to address the issues?
- Are there any policies or laws that need to be revisited or changed to address needs?
- Is funding needed? If so, what could it be used for?
- How might future community engagement help address the issues?

FINAL REFLECTION PAPER

Traditionally, instructors assign a final reflection paper to demonstrate overall learning. Papers of this type usually ask preservice ESOL teachers to revisit the initial goals they set for themselves prior to the service-learning experience and determine the extent to which they were achieved. Alternatively, they may ask preservice teachers to reflect on the most meaningful part(s) of the experience in terms of their development in each of the goal areas.

To be most meaningful in terms of transformative learning, preservice teachers should be encouraged to state not just what they learned from the service-learning experience, but how their personal beliefs or assumptions may have changed and how this will impact their future practice and goals. Depending on the context, preservice teachers might have a choice of writing this final reflection collaboratively or using a multimodal format (see Chapter 6).

Points for Reflection
- What tools or strategies do/would you use to facilitate reflective practice *after* service-learning?
- Consider the most important goals and objectives in your TESOL service-learning context; what prompts might you use for a final reflection assignment?

ARTISTIC OR CREATIVE PROJECTS

Some TESOL service-learning projects conclude with a final showcase or presentation or publication of learning. These typically comprise creative activities that celebrate successes. For example, TESOL preservice teachers may compile a booklet of selected EL work, photos, and positive reflections about the participants in the service-learning project, or they could work with ELs to organize a symposium or gallery walk in which the ELs present their work to parents and community members. Alternatively, the preservice teachers could create live or recorded presentations reflecting on the experience, which could be shared with community members; or they might write articles reflecting on the experience, which could be published in community newsletters. While these kinds of reflection do not typically involve critical reflection, they can work towards raising the profile of community needs and how service-learning can help to address them.

To extend the learning further, preservice teachers can be encouraged to build on their experience by writing up their work for academic publication or conference presentation. For an example of a TESOL presentation about a service-learning experience shared at a virtual undergraduate symposium, see https://www.youtube.com/watch?v=qfQHLMalFG8&t=1s.

REFLECTION WITH THE COMMUNITY PARTNER

One sometimes neglected reflection task at the end of a service-learning experience is a collaborative reflection with the community partner. Preservice ESOL teachers could meet with the EL teachers in the school face-to-face or virtually to reflect together on the experience. This could be done orally or in writing, formally or informally, using specific targeted prompt questions or more general evaluative prompts. A catalyst for a reflective discussion could simply be a question, like *Has this service-learning experience made a difference? If so, how? If not, why not?* Note that this is somewhat different from a program evaluation that focuses on visible benefits, costs, and logistical details. The main focus of the reflection is the extent to which needs were addressed, the effectiveness of the ESOL preservice-teachers' involvement, issues that may have emerged or existing issues that may have been revealed, and ways that the service-learning project might be improved in future.

MONITOR AND PROVIDE FEEDBACK
THROUGHOUT THE REFLECTION PROCESS

Clearly, reflections are crucial in service-learning, but assessing reflections can be problematic. Issues of assessment and feedback are discussed in Chapter 3, and sample rubrics are provided there, but I would like to reiterate the importance of including multiple opportunities for reflection and feedback in various formats. There are several reasons for this. First, the more opportunities there are to reflect and learn from feedback, the more practiced participants can become in reflection. Second, the more reflection opportunities there are, the greater the chance that evidence of learning in the target areas will be displayed. Third, the more types of reflections there are, the better the chance that participants will find the type of reflection that works best for them. The reality is that the amount of work that preservice teachers put into their reflection tasks is often correlated to grades, but opportunities for ungraded reflection, such as informal oral debriefings, peer group discussions, or quick writes are useful. Though no grades are awarded for these reflections, formative feedback in the form of oral or written comments should be provided regularly. One way to address the challenge of a heavy marking load is to include self and peer evaluation.

PROMOTING A CULTURE OF REFLECTIVE PRACTICE IN TESOL SERVICE-LEARNING

Eyler (2002a) asserts that "[s]tudents who develop these habits of reflection have the tools to get the most out of their current studies and to use for future problem solving in the community" (p. 525). So, let's revisit our earlier question, can reflective practice be cultivated in TESOL service-learning so that it becomes a natural process/action for ESOL teachers and not just an added burden for overworked teachers? Providing frequent opportunities for reflection is a start. When cycles of reflection and feedback are a regular practice in service-learning, they can more easily become a habit. Recalling that dialogue and discussion are part of the reflective process, communities of practices should be established. Dialogue with peers promotes the sharing of ideas, alternative perspectives, additional insights, and constructive feedback. Collaborative approaches are also recommended by Farrell (2019) who has some suggestions for promoting a culture of reflective practice in ELT contexts. His suggestions include teaching portfolios and self and peer assessment related to teacher appraisal/evaluation, mentoring, peer coaching, critical friends, team teaching, action research. Preservice teachers can be encouraged to continue their reflective practice through such approaches after the service-learning project is finished. They might also be encouraged to continue to participate in community engagement projects and service-learning experiences and learn more through such activities as community and professional newsletters, websites, professional development, or publishing (professional and academic journals).

TIPS FOR FACILITATING EFFECTIVE REFLECTIONS

- Make reflective practice ongoing rather than limiting it to the end. Include multiple opportunities for guided reflection before, during, and after the service-learning experience.
- Be explicit in instructions and expectations – for example: *You must cite relevant language learning theory that supports your claims and actions.*
- Encourage preservice teachers to identify both positive and negative events so that effective skills, approaches, and techniques can be highlighted for future consideration, and ineffective skills, approaches, and techniques can be marked for improvement.
- Structure reflection through interactions in various modes. Encourage feedback.
- Continually ask the questions, "why?" and "how", such as *Why do you think this happened? Why is this surprising? Why did/didn't this work? How will you use what you have learned?*
- Encourage preservice teachers to include specific examples to support claims made in reflections. It is much more credible to claim that *Ali's pronunciation was clearer after spending time working on distinguishing /p/ and /b/,* than it is to claim simply that *Ali's pronunciation improved after service-learning.*
- Warn preservice teachers to avoid generalizations and hyperbole. For example, it is unlikely that preservice teachers will learn what it is like to be an EL (unless they actually were an EL themselves).
- Engage their metacognition by having preservice teachers revisit goals and early reflections to track progress and build on.
- Encourage preservice teachers not to be afraid to reflect critically and challenge the status quo. Sometimes it is *because* preservice teachers lack experience that they can see issues where others may have become too comfortable to question.

CONCLUSION

This chapter has provided some tools and strategies for facilitating and assessing reflections before, during, and after TESOL service-learning experiences. What works in one context may not work in another, so they are offered only as a guide and should be adapted or replaced to suit specific contexts and align with target service-learning goals and objectives. Participants arrive with different levels of experience and learning styles, and developing effective reflective practice requires time, so instructors should not be discouraged if preservice ESOL teachers do not meet expectations in one service-learning experience. It is hoped that the tools and strategies here will inspire instructors to create ways to facilitate effective reflections in their contexts. In the next chapter samples of authentic reflections will be examined to determine what we can learn from them.

Chapter 5

Learning from Reflections in TESOL Service-Learning

INTRODUCTION

As discussed in Chapter 2, reflection is a way for us to make experiences meaningful in our lives (Rogers, 2002) and the benefits can be numerous. Reflection on service-learning enables us to develop our knowledge, skills, beliefs, attitudes, and civic responsibilities, and reflecting with others can deepen our understanding, open our minds, and broaden our perspectives.

In this chapter, we look more closely at various excerpts from reflections in a TESOL service-learning project to determine what might be learned from them. The reflection excerpts are discussed in terms of relevant service-learning goals for development, but it is not just preservice teachers who can learn from reflections. TESOL course instructors and community partners can learn valuable insights from reflections that can provide insight into an individual's thinking and progress, as well as information about what works and what does not work in the service-learning experience. This can inform instruction and guide future planning decisions to improve learning.

TESOL SERVICE-LEARNING CONTEXT

First, some context is needed. Several years ago, I started implementing a service-learning project in an undergraduate TESOL methods course that I teach at a US university. Some of the preservice teachers in this course are education majors, while others major in a range of disciplines, like foreign language, communication, psychology, business, and so on. The service-learning project involves working with community partners at a local low-income elementary school where a need to provide additional support for young ELs has been identified. The aim is to support the ELs' development of English literacy as well as to promote positive attitudes toward learning English. Together, we discuss ideas and arrange an after-school literacy program to be designed and implemented by the preservice ESOL teachers. The format involves three groups of preservice teachers: one small group teaches on a particular day, one group scaffolds ELs one-to-one or in small groups, and the third group observes and takes notes. Regardless of their role on a particular day, all preservice teachers are required to write reflections in their weekly journal, participate in debriefing discussions, and complete other reflection tasks.

Early on, I could see that the majority of reflections on the service-learning experience submitted by the preservice teachers were vague, lacked insight, and sometimes just seemed like a "stream of consciousness" or a rambling description of what had happened during the service-learning experience. From this, I learned that, as an instructor, I needed to help the preservice teachers generate more meaningful reflections, and I needed to start by making my expectations clearer. I also learned that I had to do a better job in scaffolding reflective practice by providing tools and models with targeted prompts and I needed to provide opportunities for frequent discussion and practice.

After implementing changes in the way I facilitate reflective practice, there is still sometimes a range in the quality of reflections that the preservice ESOL teachers submit, but there is usually no misunderstanding of what reflection is, and reflections overall are more focused and meaningful.

EXAMPLES OF REFLECTIONS BEFORE SERVICE-LEARNING

To begin, we will discuss reflections that demonstrate the thinking of preservice teachers prior to the service-learning experience. In Chapter 4, prompts for facilitating initial discussions about the purpose of service-learning were presented. Now, I would like to examine some responses to those prompts. While the responses in the exchange shown in Table 5.1 are not reflections in the way that has been previously defined, they do give an indication of the preservice teachers' initial thoughts about TESOL service-learning, which can be a catalyst for further reflective dialogue.

Points for Reflection

- Did anything strike you as odd or interesting as you read the exchange in Table 5.1?
- What might you learn from the preservice teachers' responses that might inform your practice?

Table 5.1. Example of initial discussion prior to service-learning experience

1. **CM**: In this course, there is a service-learning project where we will be working with English learners at a local elementary school. What do we mean by service-learning?
2. **Preservice teacher**: doing volunteer work in the community?
3. **CM**: well, then why don't we just call it volunteer work or community service? Why is it called service-learning?
4. **Preservice teacher**: it must include learning.
5. **CM**: yes, who is learning?
6. **Preservice teacher**: the kids in the school.
7. **CM**: [pause] and ...?
8. **Preservice teacher**: us
9. **CM**: what might *you* learn?
10. **Preservice teacher**: How to teach ELs.
11. **Preservice teacher**: Or how not to teach them. [laughter]
12. **CM**: Can you expand on that? What might you learn about teaching English learners in the community that you aren't learning here in the course or from your textbook?
13. **Preservice teacher**: We get to work with actual learners.
14. **CM**: So ...?
15. **Preservice teacher**: [pause] So, we can see what they are like.
16. **CM**: [silence]
17. **Preservice teacher**: ... what their level of English is ... what they can and can't do ...
18. **Preservice teacher**: and we can build our skills in teaching.
19. **CM**: Ok, can you be more specific? What skills exactly?
20. **Preservice teacher**: [pause] how to explain English so the kids will understand.
21. **CM**: How might you connect the service-learning experience to what you are learning in the TESOL program here?
22. **Preservice teacher**: [pause] ... here we have learned about language learning and the principles of English language teaching, so with the ELs we can see if those things work in real life.
23. **CM**: mmhmm. They may or may not work because remember that context matters. In what way do you think your teaching – or the after-school program in general – will have an impact on the English learners?
24. **Preservice teacher**: Hopefully, they will improve their English.
25. **CM**: How will you know if their English is improving?
26. **Preservice teacher**: [long pause] maybe they won't make as many errors ...
27. **Preservice teacher**: or maybe they will be more confident using English.
28. **CM**: How much improvement do you think you will see in 4 weeks [8 sessions]?
29. **Preservice teacher**: I don't know.
30. **CM**: To what extent do you think you might learn about the education system or the facilities or resources that the ELs and their families have access to?
31. **Preservice teacher**: yeah, we will see their classroom and we can ask M. [the EL teacher in the school] questions about that.

(Continued.)

32. **CM**: Besides working with learners on their English, what other contributions might you make?

33. **Preservice teacher**: maybe we can just give them some individual attention 'cause maybe during the day their teachers don't always have time.

34. **CM**: mmhmm. What might you learn from the English learners themselves?

35. **Preservice teacher**: [silence]

36. **CM**: How are you the same or different from the children we will be working with?

37. **Preservice teacher**: We speak English, and we are older and know the culture here, and they are still learning.

38. **CM**: It sounds like you will have a lot to share with them. What about the English learners? What might they share with you? ... What might you learn from them?

39. **Preservice teacher**: maybe we'll learn something about their culture that we didn't know before?

40. **CM**: Yes, maybe you will. Do you think you will learn anything about what they are good at? Or about how they learn? Or about their language or experiences or the challenges they face?

41. **Preservice teacher**: yeah.

42. **CM**: [long pause] In what way do you think our being there might have a negative impact?

43. **Preservice teacher**: [long silence]

44. **Preservice teacher**: ... maybe the kids will be nervous with so many adults and native English speakers in the room.

45. **CM**: How might you use what you learn in this experience in the future?

46. **Preservice teacher**: It will give us confidence in our teaching, hopefully, and that will make us better teachers.

47. **CM**: Just in teaching?

48. **Preservice teacher**: and in working with ELs with different L1s.

49. **CM**: One of the ways you will be assessed on your service-learning is through reflection. What do you understand by reflection?

50. **Preservice teacher**: thinking about what happened during the service-learning experience.

51. **CM**: yes, that's the first step. What else?

52. **Preservice teacher**: thinking about what we learned from it.

53. **CM**: ok, anything else?

54. **Preservice teachers**: [silence]

55. **CM**: What aspects of the service-learning experience might you reflect on to demonstrate your learning in terms of your academic or professional development?

56. **Preservice teachers**: maybe language learning theories work well ...

57. **CM**: Yes. What aspects of the service-learning experience might you reflect on to demonstrate your learning in terms of your civic identity or social or personal growth?

58. **Preservice teachers**: We might learn about other cultures ...

59. **CM**: How do you interpret critical reflection?

60. **Preservice teachers**: [silence]

61. **CM**: It is ok. We will go over the expectations of critical reflections and together we will have some opportunities to reflect critically on various issues. We will also look at some models. More on that later ...

The preservice teachers participating in the discussion in Table 5.1 may have learned that service-learning is different from volunteer work, that reflection is important, and they will learn more about it as the program progresses. As instructor, the first thing I learned from this exchange was that preservice teachers might have some familiarity with service-learning but not a full understanding, so I knew it was important to work towards making sure it was understood more fully.

In line 6, the first response about who was learning was "the kids" revealing that this preservice teacher was thinking first about helping the ELs. While this is a fair response, I followed with "and ...?", and I did not return to the ELs' learning until line 32. I did this because I wanted to emphasize the point that service-learning is a mutually beneficial endeavor and I wanted to dispel any notions of a "savior complex", that is, the misinformed belief that the purpose of service-learning is to "save" people in need. To this end I tried to elicit ideas about the strengths and contributions of the ELs so that the preservice teachers wouldn't approach them with a deficit mindset.

As the discussion progressed, I realized that the responses were often quite broad — "English teaching", "improving English", "make errors", "something about culture", and simple yes/no responses. This was to be expected at this early stage as there had not yet been any specific experiences, so I did not always push for elaboration or examples as I normally might. There were a few occasions, however, when I did push because I wanted the preservice teachers to learn to build on their reflections and get used to fully explaining their thinking and justifying their claims. In lines 7, 16, and 42, I wanted to see if I could prompt them to elaborate or revise their responses by pausing or keeping silent, and in lines 12 and 19, I tried explicit follow-up questions, such as "can you expand on that?" When I didn't get a response to my question about learning from ELs (line 34), I realized that the preservice teachers needed some time to think about this, so I asked another question and then came back and rephrased the initial question in line 38. At other times I rephrased questions with added details, though this could make the questions too leading as I found in line 40, after which the preservice teachers did not elaborate.

Not surprisingly, preservice teachers were not immediately forthcoming in terms of critical reflection at this early stage. For example, they did not instantly respond to the question about how our presence might have a negative impact (line 42), though a response was ultimately elicited (line 44). This is to be expected as it takes time to develop critical reflection skills, especially when many of the TESOL students had no experience with teaching, or service-learning, or my expectations for reflection. Many individuals expressed uncertainties and anxieties in early discussions and reflections, which reveals honesty and willingness to expose vulnerability. Such reflections provide a useful starting point for preservice teachers to revisit at the end of the service-learning experience when reflecting on their overall progress.

I was able to reassure preservice teachers that such feelings were common and that there would be support and guidance for them along the way.

EXAMINATION OF REFLECTION EXCERPTS FROM MY TESOL SERVICE-LEARNING PROJECT

Below, I present for examination 12 selected reflection excerpts from journals and assignments submitted by the preservice teachers in my TESOL course (their names and gendered pronouns are omitted for confidentiality). As excerpts, rather than full reflections, contextual information may be vague, and full alignment with reflection models, like those presented in Chapters 3 and 4, are not included. Before identifying what I consider to be evidence of learning that the preservice teachers display in the excerpts, there is an opportunity for readers to examine and reflect on each excerpt. Learning points are discussed in reference to the service-learning goals: academic/cognitive, professional, social/civic, and personal development. In addition, where relevant, comments are made about how the information from the reflection excerpts inform my instruction and feedback to preservice teachers so that I can improve my teaching and preservice teachers can continue to develop their reflection skills.

Excerpt 1

> *The most difficult time I had though, was getting them to notice what they were doing. When it is on a one-on-one level how do I get students to notice the language changes they are making to their writing or know that they're actually learning without explicitly telling them? Should I explicitly tell them or does that awareness happen when I give them praise for the cool questions they asked and the interesting sentence they wrote? I think awareness of their progress can be done through assessment at a larger scale in a big classroom where a student will realize what they did right or wrong when they get a test or quiz back. But how do I make them realize that they are learning?* (journal entry)

Points for Reflection
- What learning does the preservice teacher display in reflection excerpt 1?

In reflection excerpt 1, the preservice teacher is asking questions about how to help the ELs become more cognizant of their language learning progress and how to help them notice aspects of language. This reveals that the preservice teacher has learned the importance of noticing. This is an implicit reference to coursework where we discussed the importance of scaffolding, interaction, and noticing (SIN framework, Shapiro et al., 2014). Connecting coursework and the service experience relates to the service-learning goal of academic development. Excerpt 1 also shows that the preservice teacher understands the importance of metacognition for learning, which relates to the goal of cognitive development. By asking questions and considering different courses of action, this preservice teacher also demonstrates that they are familiar with an important stage in the reflection process that opens up space for further learning. Such questions could be used as prompts for a class or group discussion and for further reflection.

Excerpt 2

> *Anther way that differentiation in instruction was carried out was by requiring students to write different amounts depending on their proficiency level (Fairbairn & Jones-Vo, 2010). For example, the intermediate high students usually had to write more sentences, while the intermediate low students would be given sentence frames where they just had to fill in the blanks before transferring the entire product to their journal.* (final reflection paper)

Points for Reflection
- What learning does the preservice teacher display in reflection excerpt 2?

Similar to excerpt 1, the preservice teacher who wrote excerpt 2 demonstrates that they have learned how to connect the service-learning experience to TESOL coursework in a relevant way. In this reflection excerpt, the preservice teacher includes an explicit citation in reference to their claim about differentiated instruction. They also support their claim with an example, and use appropriate APA formatting for the citation, revealing that they understand academic conventions. This is another example related to the service-learning goal of academic development.

Excerpt 3

> *Using their own hands as a manipulative to associate with the five W's is a genius idea that I cannot wait to implement in my future classroom! Not only was it building on their background knowledge (SIOP), it was also giving them an aid to support using the five W's that they will always have with them.* (journal entry)

> **Points for Reflection**
> • What learning does the preservice teacher display in reflection excerpt 3?

In excerpt 3, the preservice teacher is reflecting on some peers' teaching. The preservice teacher who wrote it reveals that they have learned a teaching technique from their peers' lesson, and they are thinking about adopting it in their own future practice. They show that they recognize the importance of using gestures to scaffold language learning, and by referring to SIOP (Echevarría et al., 2017), the preservice teacher shows that they can connect TESOL coursework and the service-learning experience. This short excerpt thus touches on multiple goals: social development (learning from peers), academic development (theory–practice links), and professional development (ELT competencies).

Excerpt 4

Having the sentence frames for this lesson was extremely helpful, though it seemed like the sentence frames were too constrictive. It did not allow the ELs to fully be able to express their thoughts because the sentence frames were focusing more on just words instead of whole phrases. Differentiation is key so higher level learners could have produced more language without the sentence frames while lower level learners needed them for support but they are both accomplishing the same task with the same support. (journal entry)

> **Points for Reflection**
> • What learning is the preservice teacher demonstrating in reflection excerpt 4?

The preservice teacher who wrote excerpt 4 is reflecting on the use of sentence frames by peers. The writer demonstrates that they have learned the importance of differentiation and likes the use of sentence frames for support, but they critique the use of sentence frames for *all* learners, showing that they understand the need for differentiation. Reference to the concept of differentiation would relate to the service-learning goal of academic development, but excerpt 4 focuses more on implementing differentiation as a teaching competency, which relates to the goal of professional development. The reflection excerpt also reveals that the preservice teacher is evaluating peers in a constructive way and considering alternative approaches, which shows cognitive development. They also reveal their belief that the ELs can produce more language on their own and should not be limited. I might encourage this preservice teacher to share this reflection with their peers as feedback to foster further learning and social development.

Excerpt 5

Taking this course, and teaching this lesson affirmed to me that I want to stay where I am in education. Another education class I took this semester made me feel as if I was not capable of being a teacher, but this class makes me feel as if the opposite is true. I am excited to be a teacher. I love finding creative ways to teach concepts that engage and excite students to learn and pursue language. After observing and working with these students, this experience has only solidified my love of language and teaching. (final reflection – narration in multimodal project)

Points for Reflection

- What learning is the preservice teacher demonstrating in reflection excerpt 5?

Reflection excerpt 5 conveys the preservice teacher's enthusiasm for the service-learning experience and their passion for their chosen career, which relate to the goals of social and professional development. The importance of affect for both reflective practice and for service-learning is demonstrated through the use of words *excited* and *love*. The comparison of the TESOL course with their other education courses reveals a change in mindset, which suggests open-mindedness – a positive quality for personal growth. As a summary statement at the end of a multimodal reflection project, excerpt 5 does not include specific details or supporting examples, but these were provided earlier in the multimodal presentation.

Excerpt 6

On this day I had the chance to sit back and just observe the lesson being taught. This was super helpful to be able to watch the lesson without having to engage with the students. While working with the ELs is wonderful and a great experience, being able to have a time of uninterrupted observation gives you a new perspective in the classroom. It also allowed me to know what things I should be looking for when I teach on Wednesday ... I was also able to see how these teachers developed their lessons and get ideas for what things I would want to implement in my future classroom and what things I would have done differently if I was the teacher. For example, I loved the integration of the song and the hand motions that went along with it as a way to help students learn the way to edit their writing. However, I would have chosen a different acronym because it got some snickers from the class. (journal entry)

> **Points for Reflection**
> • What learning is the preservice teacher demonstrating in reflection excerpt 6?

In excerpt 6, the preservice teacher reflects on what was learned from observing peers, namely, a *new perspective*, increased perception, and effective teaching ideas, which relate to social, academic, and professional development goals. Some specific examples are shared near the end, as the preservice teacher demonstrates thinking about using songs and gestures as effective teaching techniques in the future. Excerpt 6 and similar reflections on peer observations provide useful information for the instructor because they confirm that the observation component is valued and should continue to be included in the service-learning experience.

Excerpt 7

> *I was talking with M's mom. She was really thankful for what we did. M was teaching me a word of Arabic before he left and his mom heard him and then she taught me how to say I love you which I thought was super sweet. I am so happy I got to work with M and really sad we aren't going back again.* (journal entry)

> **Points for Reflection**
> • What learning is the preservice teacher demonstrating in reflection excerpt 7?
> • What feedback might you give in response to this reflection?

At first glance, it appears that excerpt 7 might not provide much evidence of learning, as it is short and focused on affect (*happy, sad, sweet*) without much detail. I include it here, however, because it is a reflection that explicitly refers to language diversity in a positive way. The fact that the preservice teacher enjoyed having the EL teach some words of their language suggests that they understand the need to view the EL with an asset rather than deficit lens, which aligns with the service-learning goals of social development in terms of raising awareness of and support for diversity and showing openness to others. It is noticeable that excerpt 7 was referring to the final day of the project; nevertheless, feedback could be provided to this preservice teacher to suggest ways that the reflection could be improved, such as including more explicit details about what was learned from this interaction and about the contributions and strengths of ELs, reasons for the feelings, and ideas on how EL teaching might be implemented in future lessons.

Excerpt 8

The students were more proficient than I was expecting and also very excited (for the most part) to be working with us. I was also surprised by how proud the students are of their home cultures. It was very exciting to see! When students were writing in their journals, most of the students I observed wrote or drew something from their home culture. (reflection journal)

Points for Reflection
- What learning is the preservice teacher demonstrating in reflection excerpt 8?
- What feedback might you give to this preservice teacher?

While reflection excerpt 8 lacks specific details and examples, the phrases *more proficient than I was expecting* and *I was surprised* suggest that reflecting on the service-learning experience compelled this preservice teacher to challenge their assumptions and change their thinking in some way, which shows learning related to the goal of personal development. Feedback could highlight this positive point, but also make some recommendations. For example, the observations about the ELs' pride in their cultures needs elaboration. Various questions could be posed for guidance if necessary, like why would ELs be so proud of their home culture? Or why would you think they wouldn't be? How might the fact that ELs *wrote or drew something from their home culture* impact future teaching and learning?

Excerpt 9

I was disappointed that more parents didn't come to the final session to see their children present what they learned in the program. I would like to learn more about the families to be able to see if they didn't come because of a language barrier, or because of work, or something else. I understand that these families face many challenges and in the future I want to somehow help the parents of my EL students feel more included. (journal entry)

Points for Reflection
- What learning is the preservice teacher demonstrating in reflection excerpt 9?

The preservice teacher who wrote excerpt 9 has learned to explore possibilities before reaching any conclusions in their reflections, and suggests several possible reasons for the parents' absence from the final session. Raising the issue of a language barrier demonstrates that this preservice teacher is aware of the lack of access for these parents – whether real or perceived. The preservice teacher shows empathy by stating "I understand that these families face many challenges" and the comment about helping families feel more included in the future means that this preservice teacher has developed an understanding of the importance of community engagement and is thinking about implications for future practice. Excerpt 9 clearly aligns with the service-learning goal for social development.

Excerpt 10

> *I don't like how we sometimes have to move from the library to the classroom to the gym and back whenever another meeting needs the space. This lack of continuity about where we will be each day shows that the ELs are the lowest priority for facilities and resources.* (journal entry)

> **Points for Reflection**
> - What learning is the preservice teacher demonstrating in reflection excerpt 10?
> - In what way is this excerpt different from others?

Reflection excerpt 10 demonstrates that this preservice teacher has learned to critically reflect on experiences with a social justice lens. Excerpt 10 is one of few reflections that reveals a willingness to challenge administrative decisions or policies regarding the service-learning program. This demonstrates a desire to advocate for the ELs, which aligns with the goal of social or civic development. The disapproval is clear and a valid learning point for both me and the school administrators who have the capacity to address this in future. It was rather disconcerting to realize that I was not practicing what I preached by not advocating for a more stable space for the EL after-school program. This reflection tells me that I can do more to promote advocacy work both with the preservice teachers in my course, as well as in my own practice.

Excerpt 11

> *It was so sad to leave all of the students at [this school], but I am hoping to contact the ESL teacher and maybe do some classroom observations. I have lots of observation hours in the general education classroom but I really don't have much experience with ELs. I know that the more practice I have the better teacher I will be.* (final reflection paper)

Points for Reflection
- What learning is the preservice teacher demonstrating in reflection excerpt 11?

Expressing sadness about leaving shows that the preservice teacher who wrote excerpt 11 felt positive about the experience, or the ELs, or teaching generally. Enjoyment or satisfaction in the service-learning experience, however, does not necessarily equate to learning. The comment about lacking experience and needing more practice suggests self-awareness, so it could be argued that there is some personal development. The preservice teacher explicitly refers to a desire to participate in future community engagement activities, which implies a sense of civic responsibility, but the focus on personal benefits rather than shared benefits suggests that making a contribution to the community may be secondary for this preservice teacher.

Excerpt 12

> *It was a busy, but really great last day to the program. I've loved working at [this school] so much — it's reminded me how much I love working with elementary students and has made me so excited for teaching ESL to this age group in the future! I feel like I have come out of this experience with a much better understanding of WIDA levels, as well as how to adapt activities in order to match the expectations with what students at different levels are able to produce. Although I know I still have a lot to learn about differentiation and other things, the after-school program at [this school] was an amazing place to grow as a teacher.* (journal entry)

Points for Reflection
- What learning is the preservice teacher demonstrating in reflection excerpt 12?

Reflection excerpt 12 addresses multiple service-learning goals in different growth areas. It is overly general in some parts, but the preservice teacher who wrote it acknowledges their professional growth, specifically in terms of learning the WIDA levels (WIDA is an approach to supporting and assessing multilingual learners in multiple American states), matching activities with needs, the importance of differentiated instruction, and the impact on future practice. What is very evident here are the personal feelings of excitement and passion that are revealed and then tempered by the demonstration of self-awareness (personal development) in the comment about still having a lot to learn.

SUMMARY

The preservice teachers in my TESOL methods course unanimously claimed that they enjoyed the service-learning experience. As mentioned, however, enjoyment does not necessarily represent learning. It is through examination of reflections in alignment with the target service-learning goals that evidence of learning is revealed.

In terms of academic development, learning was evident when preservice teachers made connections between language learning theory and specific events in the service-learning experience. This demonstrated a contextualization of knowledge and deeper understanding of concepts and strategies than was evident in the TESOL classroom alone. It could be argued that even in the cases where inaccuracies were revealed, the act of revisiting the academic content through reflection formed a useful part of the ongoing learning process. Interestingly, learning was also evident when preservice teachers made connections to past experiences in other programs or courses. This interconnection of knowledge manifested through reflection is further evidence of learning.

Learning related to professional skills was evident through preservice teachers' reflections about their increased confidence in their teaching competencies and greater understanding of expectations in English language teaching. These contrasted noticeably with initial reflections that revealed uncertainty and anxiety. Learning was also evident in references to their use of specific language teaching strategies and techniques and in comments about their future career goals. Critical reflection was displayed occasionally demonstrating learning beyond the immediate context, but, similar to other studies discussed in Chapter 2, these were infrequent.

In the area of social development, learning was frequently revealed by preservice teachers who reflected on ideas and techniques learned from peers through observation and collaborative discussion. Comments about receiving feedback and hearing other perspectives demonstrated not just openness to others' ideas, but also gratitude to peers for sharing knowledge and ideas that they themselves had not thought of. Peer sharing was not limited to knowledge and ideas. In oral discussions, they shared stories and challenges and frustrations and they claimed that reflecting on these shared experiences gave them support and encouragement. Interacting with ELs also had an impact on learning as several preservice teachers claimed to have improved their awareness and understanding of the abilities and needs of ELs, though fewer reflections explicitly demonstrated learning with regard to the knowledge and experience that the ELs brought with them. Reflections revealing plans for future community engagement or a sense of civic responsibility were rare.

In terms of personal growth, preservice teachers' reflections displayed increased self-awareness, revealed through the ability to identify specific gaps in their abilities, as well as areas in which they felt confident. Reflective practice provided an opportunity for preservice teachers to think about the experience and find connections to their existing knowledge in order to make sense of it and personalize the learning gained from the experience. Towards the end, positive attitudes towards the experience were common in reflections, suggesting an increased sense of personal efficacy. A few preservice teachers reflected on their changing beliefs and assumptions, indicating some evidence of transformative learning.

After facilitating awareness of the reflective process in an intentional way and providing opportunities for reflective practice, improvements could be seen in the overall quality of reflections. However, while reflections were generally more introspective than they had been in previous cohorts, the range in the quality of reflections still varied. Despite the transparency of expectations and increased levels of preparation, practice, and guidance provided, reflections sometimes lacked relevant details, supporting examples, and insight. It is possible that some preservice ESOL teachers did not internalize a clear understanding of what effective reflective practice was, or perhaps the level of comfort in sharing personal thoughts, beliefs, or values was higher for some than others. Some preservice teachers simply seemed to be addressing the expectations in a cursory way, suggesting that they did not yet know how to effectively reflect on the experience, or possibly, other commitments limited the time and effort they could devote to their reflection assignments.

While some things are beyond our control, more can be done to convince preservice teachers of the value of reflecting on service-learning and to foster a culture of reflective practice as they continue in ELT. A few preservice teachers were starting to reflect critically by considering broader sociopolitical issues when exploring underlying reasons for observed behaviors and events, but these were limited in number and in depth. Work also still needs to be done to promote transformative learning and facilitate critical reflections that address social injustices. For example, missing in reflections were meaningful discussions of the role of identity in the service-learning context, deeper awareness of the assets ELs bring, explicit intentions to advocate for ELs in future, and greater commitment to future community engagement. Adding opportunities for critical reflection to complement the more standard reflection can help expand thinking and potentially lead to more impactful learning, though it is acknowledged that developing skills in critical reflection takes time, certainly more than one semester, especially for individuals who do not have much experience with it. For my part, I will continue to systematically reflect on what I learn from the preservice teachers' reflections so that I can make informed improvements to my own practice.

CONCLUSION

This chapter examined selected reflection excerpts from preservice teachers in a service-learning project in my TESOL methods course. Examining reflection excerpts in alignment with the TESOL service-learning goals (academic/cognitive, professional, social/civic, and personal development) revealed both strengths and gaps in development, which provides insights into how and where I can improve my instruction and the type of feedback needed to help guide preservice teachers to further develop their reflective practice in TESOL service-learning going forward.

Chapter 6

Impacts of Technology on Reflective Practice in TESOL Service-Learning

INTRODUCTION

This chapter explores the ways that technology has impacted service-learning, with a particular focus on reflective practice in virtual contexts. We start by considering technology in service-learning more generally. Interestingly, the NYLC service-learning standards (2008) do not mention technology at all, likely due to the value of in-person learning in community contexts. Nevertheless, technology often plays a part in various ways in service-learning, from simply using course management systems for communicating and sharing information, to recording events on video for observation and analysis, or using internet resources in implementing and presenting service projects.

Technology also has the capacity to be transformative by shifting the focus of service-learning from the local community to the global digital community. Indeed, Waldner et al. (2010) argue that online platforms, rather than being an obstacle to service-learning, actually facilitate it because they remove the geographical constraints of experiential learning and provide more opportunities and powerful tools for interaction and shared reflection.

Points for Reflection
- In what ways do you think technology might enhance learning in TESOL service-learning contexts?
- Consider a TESOL service-learning course that you teach or plan to teach. In what ways do you/would you use technology in the course, particularly for reflective practice?

Reflective practice in service-learning has also been impacted by technology. Written reflections, traditionally submitted on paper, have typically been replaced, not only with electronically submitted written assignments and portfolios, but also with audio and video recordings and multimodal presentations. Face-to-face discussions to reflect with peers, community partners, and instructors can be supplemented with discussions on Zoom (https://zoom.us/), Google Hangouts (https://hangouts.google.com/), or other video conferencing platforms. Technology can make thinking visible in collaborative reflection activities using digital content sharing platforms that were not possible in the past, such as Google Drive (https://www.google.com/drive/), Padlet (https://padlet.com/), Voicethread (https://apps.apple.com/us/app/voicethread/id465159110), and many more.

Ideally, service-learning programs are conducted face-to-face, but as academic programs started migrating to online platforms around the world, there was a move to incorporate virtual or electronic-service-learning (e-service-learning) and, as a consequence of restrictions due to the COVID-19 pandemic, e-service-learning has attracted more attention. Research on e-service-learning, while limited, has started to increase and, to support higher education institutions as they transition to virtual forms of service-learning, the European Observatory of Service-Learning in Higher Education published a *Practical guide on e-service-learning in response to COVID-19* (Albanesi et al., n.d.). Similarly, some university service-learning centers, like Louisiana State University's Center for Community Engagement, Learning, and Leadership (Becker et al., 2020), are providing advice and resources for e-service-learning.

TYPES OF ELECTRONIC SERVICE-LEARNING

E-service-learning is "an e-learning pedagogy that involves students through technology in civic inquiry, service, reflection, and action" (Albanesi et al., n.d., p. 23). Either the service or the learning component can take place partially or completely online in various combinations or types of e-service-learning (Table 6.1): online course instruction with onsite service-learning, onsite course instruction with online service-learning, blended course instruction with blended service-learning, and online course instruction with online service-learning (Waldner et al., 2012).

After a systematic review of 19 studies of single-semester e-service-learning projects, Stefaniak (2020) claims that, regardless of the type, e-service-learning can remove geographical barriers and bring people together, promoting a sense of community and student engagement and learning. This is relevant in TESOL, where the ability to connect preservice teachers with multilingual learners around the world

Table 6.1. Types of e-service-learning (based on Waldner et al., 2012)

Traditional service-learning = onsite instruction + onsite service-learning experience			
E-service-learning Type 1	E-service-learning Type 2	E-service-learning Type 3	E-service-learning Type 4 (= Extreme e-service-learning;
online course instruction + onsite service-learning	onsite course instruction + online service-learning	blended course instruction + blended service-learning	online course instruction + online service-learning
Service e-learning = learning through service AND technology (Dailey-Hebert et al., 2008)			

can provide authentic language and cultural exchange and benefits individuals in contexts that might not otherwise have this opportunity.

Despite the geographical freedom that technology accords, Dailey-Hebert et al. (2008) caution that technology is not value neutral and the context should be carefully considered when using it as an approach to learning. This is a good point because access to technology varies, even within industrialized areas. Their notion of service-e-learning (note the different position of the "e") is "an integrative pedagogy that engages learners through technology in civic inquiry, service, reflection, and action" (p. 1) and they shift the focus from "technology as a *tool* to technology as *pedagogy*" (p. 3. their emphasis). Dailey-Hebert and Donnelli-Sallee (2010) stress that "rather than simply utilizing technologies to facilitate some facet of traditional service-learning, service-eLearning students learn through service as well as through technology, engaging in critical examination of the role of technology in facilitating academic and civic learning outcomes" (p. 221). Their emphasis on using technology *for* learning rather than simply *supporting* learning highlights the need to be more strategic in how we can use technology to meet service-learning goals and transform learning. This gives rise to questions about how effective virtual service-learning is for enhancing learning.

EFFECTIVENESS OF E-SERVICE-LEARNING

A common suggestion of many of the researchers cited in this chapter is that e-service-learning can be effective if it is planned with the appropriate use of technology, if students are given choices, and if there is frequent and ongoing communication and progress tracking. Bringle and Clayton (2020) also advise that, for digital technologies to enhance service-learning, the design of the learning experiences must include collaborative community-engaged activities and critical reflection that focus on civic outcomes and other service-learning goals, aligned with the needs of the community partner.

Online learning requires a certain level of autonomy, and challenges exist, such as the need for technological resources and support, access to materials, a disconnect between the students and the community they are serving, as well as difficulties communicating and fostering a collaborative online community. That said, Stefaniak (2020) found that, when instructors required students to actively engage with course content and with peers, they achieved higher levels of participation and autonomy. Use of reflection journals in particular helped students connect their service-learning projects to the course content and enabled instructors to give frequent feedback (p. 564). She adds that "[t]ransfer of learning can be supported through the integration of reflection activities that are strategically dispersed throughout the course to allow for students to build upon newly acquired skills and knowledge" (p. 568).

> **Points for Reflection**
> - Could e-service-learning be feasible in your context?
> - What factors would affect your decision about which type of e-service-learning to implement?
> - Do you think the integration of onsite and online environments might improve learning?

EXAMPLES OF E-SERVICE-LEARNING

E-service-learning projects are becoming more prevalent around the world. For examples, see Early and Lasker (2018), Gasper-Hulvat (2018), Guthrie and McCraken (2014), Harris (2017), Sandy and Franco (2014), Stefaniak (2020), and others. In TESOL, e-service learning examples are currently less common (see Crosby, 2017; Purmensky, 2015). Sharing examples can give us some insight into the effectiveness of approaches and techniques used, which can inform future e-service-learning projects, so I would like to highlight a few examples of e-service-learning projects that we can learn from.

Gasper-Hulvat's (2018) e-service-learning project involved art history students working remotely with the Archives of American Art in Washington, DC to edit transcripts of oral histories for web publication. Gasper-Hulvat notes the equalizing effect of e-service-learning, in that economically diverse learners did not have the expense of traveling to the service site. The reminder, here, is that access to technology by all participants and community partners needs to be established prior to the e-service-learning. An interesting contrast was identified in this project between face-to-face and online service-learning, whereby live interactions elicited immediate feelings of discomfort, disagreement, and confrontation, while online participants had more control (and time) to pause, process, ignore, or structure a response. In contrast, Waldner et al. (2012) view live interactions in a positive way and raise potential problems of online meetings, such as loss of spontaneity, face-to-face group dynamics, and critical networking. Given the importance of collaborative dialogue in reflective practice, these factors are relevant considerations when planning e-service-learning experiences.

> **Points for Reflection**
> - To facilitate reflection in a TESOL service-learning context, consider the circumstances in which you might apply either of these approaches:
>   - Participants share reflections through live dialogue (in person or synchronously online), potentially resulting in spontaneity, positive group dynamics, sharing of real-time feelings.
>   - Participants reflect on online discussion boards or through audio recordings, potentially resulting in higher comfort levels, more thoughtful/considered responses.

Early and Lasker (2018) stress the value of collaboration in their online service-learning work in a global health course. They found that, in addition to offering students choice and maintaining strong communication, "providing platforms for collaboration (e.g., online work groups, social media) will strengthen social presences and build community online that aids community building offline" (p. 224). Building a collaborative online community is also important for fostering discussion as part of the reflective process in e-service-learning. For example, Smit and Tremethick (2017) found that online group reflection after international service-learning experiences in nursing education resulted in more topics being raised and more reflective thinking being demonstrated than in the individual written reflections. They conclude that online group discussion could be implemented as a teaching strategy to facilitate critical reflection.

Participants also found collaborative dialogue helpful for reflection in Guthrie and McCracken's (2014) study of e-service-learning. Students from a range of disciplines valued the reflective process because its collaborative dialogue helped them see diverse perspectives and enhance their critical thinking. Structured questions regarding community engagement, social issues, lifelong learning, and making positive change guided ongoing discussions in online forums, web-based journals, asynchronous threaded discussions, reflection essays, and position papers throughout the reflection process. The authors stress that "[r]eflection must be a guided process in order for its results to be consistent with institutional goals, viewed as academically viable as well as individually meaningful" (p. 248). They caution, however, that students may be less forthcoming in sharing their reflections with peers in large online classes. Motivation to participate in virtual settings is discussed in more detail later.

The benefits of technology for collaborative or shared reflection in terms of reaching a wider audience and deepening the meaning-making process are recognized by Bringle and Clayton (2020). They give the example of digital story-telling, which, when clearly linked to learning objectives, is a way that participants can construct meaning by publicly exploring events experienced during service, connecting them with academic experiences, engaging in group interactions to raise issues and ask questions, and creating ways to convey ideas creatively while incorporating academic integrity. Critically reflecting through digital story-telling has the benefit of helping students learn "about the responsible use of technology … expand[s] their use of technology to creatively approach and contribute to civic and social issues in communities, and [guides them in] using collaborative technologies to improve communication skills with diverse others and examine issues from multiple perspectives" (p. 57). Digital story-telling could be a fun and beneficial way to reflect in TESOL e-service-learning contexts.

Points for Reflection

- The studies highlighted here stress the importance of building a collaborative online community and engaging in collaborative dialogue for reflection in e-service-learning. Consider what some of the challenges might be, how you might encourage online collaboration in an e-service-learning context, and how those challenges might be addressed.

Sharing reflections with groups using digital platforms widens the reach of ideas and can help instructors "and their students all contribute to one another's learning and growth" (Bringle & Clayton, 2020, p. 58). Nevertheless, there are some issues to consider when integrating technology in service-learning and reflective practice.

ADDRESSING CHALLENGES OF REFLECTIVE PRACTICE USING TECHNOLOGY

Facilitating reflection in e-service-learning is not without its challenges, of course. Access to technology and technical support are real obstacles. It is important to ensure that the use of technology does not intensify existing inequalities in the community or amongst participants. It should increase access and enhance learning, not limit it. Online platforms and tools must be planned with community partners and agreed upon together with e-service-learning participants. Repositories can be set up to share and maintain organization of materials and reflections.

Related to this, instructors' lack of familiarity with and level of confidence using technology can be a deterrent. While this may be true, there will no doubt always be a range in the levels of digital literacy and comfort amongst participants working with technology; yet this doesn't have to be a problem. In my experience, TESOL preservice teachers are happy to raise each other's awareness of digital tools and teach peers, community partners, and me how to use them. In addition, technology experts can be brought into virtual sessions to provide training in relevant tools, and/or online tutorials can be used. Of course, instructors need to plan time for training opportunities, as well as time for students to practice using the tools.

Other issues can also arise. Simply transferring a traditional reflection activity to an online format may not work. Instructors need to consider how reflection activities and assignments align to service-learning objectives in a virtual platform and, if they don't, time is needed to redesign them. Notably, platforms for communication and communication tasks need to be designed in a way that supports learning as interaction is crucial for reflective practice (Rogers, 2002; Farrell, 2019). Indeed, facilitating effective online communication is an issue that emerges frequently in the literature. For example, Pawan et al. (2016) report on a study of an online professional development program for ESOL and content area teachers where "collaborative reflections were hindered by the online instructors' failure to always provide an appropriate task structure" (p. 22) and this led to various problems, like lack of opportunity for peer interactions, or "serial monologues" where participants shared reflections on their experiences online but made little effort "to connect to and integrate the contributions of others" (p. 21). To address these problems, weekly moderating roles were assigned to participants to compel them to elicit greater collaboration. For example, in the "starter role", participants would draw on previous discussions to design a reflection prompt and identify connections between peers' contributions. In the "provocateur role", participants would challenge peers to elaborate and clarify their reflections and identify contradictions, as well as connections, ideas, resources, and so on. In the "wrapper role", participants would summarize the reflections on the initial prompt and synthesize ideas to move everyone to a new level of understanding. Essential aspects of this process include the regularity (weekly) and the student-centeredness which can lead to greater engagement and collaboration.

Another issue that can arise with reflective practice in a virtual environment, as mentioned earlier regarding e-service-learning generally, is a feeling of isolation. Lack of face-to-face interaction and too much screen time can lead to a lack of engagement, and boredom. To address this, it is important to include a variety of interactive reflection activities (both synchronous and asynchronous), make sure they are student-centered, and limit the duration of tasks. Albanesi et al. (n.d.) asserts that in e-service-learning "maintaining active and constructive communication is key. The instructors must remain actively engaged from the beginning to the end of the project, giving continuous feedback and offering space for reflection" (p. 35).

One tip I have learned – for both face-to-face and online classes – is to break instruction up with quick and regular "processing" breaks. After about ten minutes of "teacher talk", students can take one to two minutes or more to write down and then discuss with peers their thoughts (reflections) about the application of an academic concept or a learning point regarding the service experience. Online chat, breakout rooms, Google Docs (https://www.google.com/docs/about/), or online polls can be used for this. Doing this regularly and mixing up the use of pairs, small groups, and whole groups for sharing gives participants time to clarify and process concepts, explore ideas and others' perspectives on them, and work towards deeper understanding. These interactions can help alleviate feelings of isolation and boredom and spark ideas. For longer interactions and responses to more structured prompts, collaborative writing platforms like Google Docs can be set up. Monitoring written responses in real time makes participants' thinking visible. Alternatively, resources like Flip (https://info.flip.com/) allow participants to video record their thoughts and then give and receive feedback from peers. These are just a few of the ways that technology can be used in the reflective process.

Garrison and Kanuka (2004) make the point that, while face-to-face or synchronous online interactions can promote energy and enthusiasm, this form of discourse can sometimes be superficial, irrelevant, lacking in thought, and ineffective for learning. In contrast, asynchronous interactions "facilitate a simultaneous independent and collaborative learning experience. That is, learners can be independent of space and time – yet together" (p. 97). Indeed, I have noticed in my experience that some participants feel less intimidated in an online discussion –whether synchronous or asynchronous – than they do face-to-face. Perhaps the virtual platform and distance provide some sense of anonymity or perhaps perceived negative aspects of face-to-face interactions can be diminished, such as intimidation based on physical presence and sensory cues, like encroachment into someone's "comfort zone", vocal volume, gestures, even style of clothing and perfume. While online sharing can lead to more honest reflections, there is also a risk that individual biases, deficit-oriented views, or justifications for existing inequities can emerge and be amplified due to "online disinhibition" (Becker et al., 2020). Bringle and Clayton (2020) address this point when they claim, "With often less explicit dynamics of power and privilege – so visible in the face-to-face classroom – and often with time to formulate and refine ideas, some students may feel freer not only to participate but to challenge others' ideas in virtual spaces, a key aspect of both community building and learning in virtual spaces that may transfer to face-to-face contexts as well" (p. 55).

These challenges are important considerations when implementing reflection tasks in online platforms. Such tasks should be planned in a sensitive way and it may be helpful to establish working agreements that include constructive ways to challenge peers' contributions.

Importantly, asynchronous communication can provide the time to reflect more deeply and "confront questionable ideas and faulty thinking in more objective and reflective ways than might be possible in a face-to-face context" (Garrison & Kanuka, 2004, p. 99). This is something, as Garrison and Kanuka argue, that students rarely do in isolation yet is important for developing critical reflection and metacognition. To this end, it is crucial to build a "community of inquiry" (Garrison et al., 2010). Their community of inquiry framework, which has been reviewed and validated through multiple studies, has three essential and intersecting elements: *teaching presence*, *cognitive presence*, and *social presence*. It was originally developed for e-learning, yet very smoothly applies to e-service-learning as well. *Cognitive presence* refers to reflective inquiry based on connecting educational experience and service. *Teacher presence* refers to the need for effective design of learning experiences with continuous facilitation, direction, and feedback. *Social presence* refers to the need for a space in which students can regularly and freely engage in critical discussion of service-learning experiences. Here, a safe online environment enables instructors to facilitate discussions and help students learn to question beliefs and challenge norms.

As with traditional forms of service-learning, it is important to provide regular opportunities to reflect, but be aware that reflection fatigue can become a potential problem, especially in online contexts. This can be avoided by strategically selecting reflection tasks that vary in terms of focus and prompts, as well as approach, mode, and complexity, such as individual and collaborative, one-off and continuous, graded and ungraded, written, oral, multimodal. It is also crucial to set reflection tasks and assignments in advance and make instructions and expectations transparent from the beginning.

Points for Reflection

- Do you think that online platforms would generally help or hinder communication in TESOL service-learning contexts? Are online platforms safer or more intimidating places for preservice ESOL teachers to reflect on learning in your view?
- How might virtual environments affect perceptions of, and reflection on, community experiences?
- How might virtual platforms affect conceptions of, and reflection on, social justice issues and need for social change?

SAMPLE FORMATS OF VIRTUAL REFLECTIONS OR TECHNOLOGY SUPPORTED REFLECTIONS

Some common formats of virtual reflections are outlined below but this list is not exhaustive, nor is it meant to prescribe a particular format. Example prompts are not included here as contexts vary widely.

Virtual Dialogue

Virtual dialogue on video-conferencing platforms can involve structured or unstructured interactions and should be set up frequently, and, like all tasks, have a relevant purpose. For example, the purpose of informal sharing sessions might be to build community and debrief after service experiences, or to check on social emotional well-being and exchange coping strategies. This is particularly important for e-service-learning communities, where participants never meet in person. More structured dialogue should be designed regularly and intentionally with the purpose of collaborative reflection, with opportunities to share experiences, suggest interpretations, analyze ideas and perspectives, and explore issues that arise. Specific prompts can be provided to guide discussions and encourage participants to make connections, broaden issues, give and receive feedback. As Pawan et al. (2016) report, weekly monitoring roles can be assigned and rotated so participants have the responsibility of developing prompts and guiding reflection themselves. Another way to guide discussions is by using collaborative writing tools, like Google Docs and shared screen features on Zoom, as well as online chat. Prompts and reporting templates can be set up in advance and instructors can monitor them in real time. The instructor may or may not join discussion groups to observe or give feedback, though their presence should be made evident in other ways, such as commenting on the collaborative writing. Dialogues can be one-off or cyclical depending on the context. Group size will also depend on context and task.

E-journals, Blogs, and Vlogs

E-journals, weblogs (blogs), and videologs (vlogs) are an asynchronous way to reflect virtually on the service-learning experience. The benefit of e-journals, blogs, and vlogs over traditional reflection journals is that images, audio and video texts can be incorporated, which allows for greater choices and creativity, which can increase motivation. In addition, strategically incorporated visuals can sometimes represent thinking more effectively than text. Note that permissions should be sought first before using copyrighted images or photos or video of peers or community partners. In an interesting study comparing weekly blog and vlog reflection posts on preservice teacher fieldwork, Kajder and Parkes (2012) found that blogs tend to focus more on surface level reflections of content, whereas vlogs tend to include higher levels of reflection that documented learning.

E-journals, blogs, and vlogs can also easily be shared electronically with peers, community partners, and beyond, and used as a basis for discussion and learning from different perspectives. For example, participants in an international service-learning internship in East Africa maintained blogs that were publicly accessible on a website (Larsen, 2014). Using these kinds of platforms allows the use of images and other modalities of expression, which can potentially be more engaging for viewers. If privacy is an issue, they can be shared with the class and/or the instructor only. Regardless, regular opportunities should be provided for this kind of reflection and instructor and/or peer feedback should be given. One popular platform for vlogs is Flip where participants can record themselves reflecting briefly on an experience and share it with others who can reply with written or video comments within the platform.

Online Discussion Boards

Online discussion boards allow for shared reflections in a way that eliminates the pressures that some participants may feel in synchronous interactions as there is time for more thoughtful reflection. Averett and Arnd-Caddigan (2014) claim that "some students will post thoughts on more controversial topics and have more open discussion when given the perceived 'safety' of an online discussion board" (p. 326). TESOL service-learning instructors can direct threaded discussions through prompts that link to course readings and impel participants to make connections between TESOL coursework and the service experiences, as well as to issues that arise in peers' contributions.

E-portfolios

E-portfolios are useful for compiling and displaying different reflection artifacts together with evidence of learning over time. Participants express their individual style in how they choose to display their reflections. For example, claims made in reflections can be illustrated with samples of EL work, lesson plans, teaching materials, visuals, or even audio recordings and videoclips of actions. Written or recorded narration can highlight strategic learning points to help viewers navigate the e-portfolio. Perhaps the greatest benefit of e-portfolios, besides the personalized content, is that growth over time can be demonstrated in more flexible ways and supported with evidence in multiple modes.

Alternative Means of Virtual Reflection

There are other forms of reflection that could be adapted to virtual platforms. These can include e-posters, artwork, poetry, synchronous or video-recorded role plays, multimodal presentations, and so on. Artistic expression taps into the emotional aspects of service-learning experiences and can be a powerful means of reflection. Averett and Arnd-Caddigan (2014) claim that "art, by its very nature, engages in social issues and in the creation of social change. As well, student responses to art involve emotional dimensions and engagement in critical reflection" (p. 327). They suggest, as examples, identity collages or artistic representations of self or of culture to prompt further reflection on personal or group identity and behaviors.

Points for Reflection
- In your current or future TESOL service-learning context, what formats of virtual reflections do/would you use and why?
- Can you think of reflection prompts that might be more suitable for one format over another?

SAMPLE MULTIMODAL REFLECTION ASSIGNMENT IN TESOL SERVICE-LEARNING

A final reflection assignment that I assign to my undergraduate preservice ESOL teachers in their service-learning experience provides a multimodal reflection option. It is assessed and accounts for a substantial part of the grade because it is the final assignment after they have had multiple opportunities for discussion and several cycles of reflection and feedback on smaller, ungraded reflection tasks. For this final reflection assignment, preservice teachers in my TESOL course have a choice of reflection artifact; they can create a multimodal presentation reflecting on the service-learning experience or they can write a reflection paper. They may also choose to work with a partner or independently. Providing more options and choices gives participants increased agency. There are set criteria to meet, and guidelines (see Table 6.2) and rubric are provided in advance. In addition, models from previous cohorts could be shared (after gaining permission).

The rubric for the multimodal reflection would be adapted from the Rubric for the Final Reflection presented in Table 3.2 in Chapter 3. It would be shared with the preservice teachers along with the assignment guidelines.

Table 6.2. Final reflection assignment guidelines: multimodal or written format

---

You will create a written OR multimodal reflection on your service-learning experience. You have the choice of doing this assignment alone or with a partner. It is an academic reflection, so, regardless of the format you choose, evidence of scholarship is required. This means you must cite at least three different language learning scholars who have informed your practice or beliefs.

Your reflection should include:

- A brief description of the overall experience including selected examples of SPECIFIC challenges and successes.
- An examination of the factors that made these experiences challenging or successful, and suggestions of alternative actions where applicable.
- An articulation of what you learned in terms of development goals (academic/cognitive, professional, social/civic, & personal). Importantly, you should also consider how this experience will impact your future practice & goals.

Use the rubric to guide your reflection. As you reflect, keep in mind four development goals:

- Academic/cognitive: what you have learned about ESOL teaching in the coursework, including language learning theory and principles, etc. Reflect on how this impacted your service-learning experience.
- Professional: ESOL teaching competences that you feel confident about and those you still need to improve. Consider what being an ESOL teacher in this context is like, what you learned about the profession, etc.
- Social/civic: what you have learned from interactions with ELs, peers, community partners. Consider issues of cultural and linguistic diversity, other peoples' perspectives, how to work as a team, what it is like to give and receive feedback, etc.
- Personal: what you have learned about yourself, e.g. your cultural awareness, ability to empathize, ability to critically reflect, your beliefs about ESOL teaching and learning, your attitude about community engagement and civic responsibility, etc.

This reflection will demonstrate progress over the whole program; however, it should highlight specific incidents or events. Compare these reflection excerpts:

Excerpt A	Excerpt B
During this service-learning experience, I used a lot of SIOP strategies to scaffold learning and now I feel more confident as an ESOL teacher.	*At first I was frustrated because I was trying to build on Khalil's (pseudonym) existing knowledge of sentence structures and even provided some sentence frames, but he wouldn't even try to write his sentence. It wasn't until I discovered that he didn't feel comfortable sitting with the other boys at his table that I realized his lack of effort was probably not related to his writing ability. Looking beyond academics to social or cultural issues and figuring out how to address them will make me a better ESOL teacher.*

(Continued)

Don't simply create a list of things you learned. Think about the events or incidents that were the most meaningful or had the most impact on you. Describe these, examine them carefully, say what you learned from them and why this is significant going forward.

Some requirements:

- For a written reflection, use Times New Roman, Font size 12, single spaced
  - o Write 2000–2500 words excluding reference list.
  - o Use appropriate headings for reader friendliness.
- For a multimodal presentation, create a narrated slideshow or video using software of your choice.
  - o The presentation will be about three minutes depending on whether you work individually or with a partner.
  - o If you work with a partner, each of you must contribute equally to the narration, i.e. approximately 1.5 minutes of narration each. You can alternate slides, or one can narrate the first half, while the other narrates the last half. Either way, try to integrate your reflections somehow to make a cohesive whole.
  - o Start with a title slide with your names in full.
  - o Be creative AND strategic in choosing photos and editing tools. They should be relevant to the narration and enhance the reflection.
- At the end of both formats of reflection, include a written reference list for the works cited (APA formatted), as well as a written acknowledgment to the ELs and the school.

Points for Reflection

- In your current or future TESOL service-learning context, is/would your final reflection assignment be similar or different to this? Why?
- Do you think the rubric for this assignment would capture the targeted learning points? How could it be improved without being too complicated to use?

RECOMMENDATIONS FOR USING TECHNOLOGY IN REFLECTION ON TESOL SERVICE-LEARNING EXPERIENCES

Informed by e-service-learning scholars and my own experience, some recommendations for using technology in reflection in TESOL service-learning are summarized here:

- First, ensure that the service-learning experience and the use of digital technology are integrated in ways that align with the goals (academic/cognitive, social/civic, professional, personal development).
- Together with the community partner, assess participants' access to technology and support.

- Ensure that reflection platforms are secure in virtual spaces, like the university's course management system.
- Create a community of inquiry (Garrison et al., 2010) by designing and facilitating intellectual, social, and emotionally safe platforms for reflection activities and collaboration. Maintain academic integrity, social interaction, and a teaching presence throughout. In some contexts, it may be useful to generate working agreements (rules of conduct) together with participants for virtual interactions.
- Ensure that instructions and expectations are clearly communicated and repeated on multiple platforms. Post models on course management systems.
- Share a variety of digital tools, like Google applications, social media platforms, wikis, video conferencing, blogs, Flip (https://info.flip.com/), Creative Cloud (https://www.adobe.com/express/), StoryCorps (https://storycorps.org/), WriteReader (https://www.writereader.com/), Screencastify (https://www.screencastify.com/), and importantly, provide live or recorded tutorials for their use. Note that best results are elicited when students are given the option to find the tools that work best for them (Stefaniak, 2020).
- Provide purposeful opportunities for ongoing dialogue between individuals, groups, and community partners through discussion boards, group forums, virtual group meetings, and collaborative writing platforms. Specific topics and prompts should include reference to application of TESOL course content in the context of service experience and issues that arise.
- Allow flexibility and choice in the use of synchronous and asynchronous platforms, digital tools, individual and collaborative reflection, assignment formats and deadlines.
- Require regular cycles of reflection and feedback through online journaling, shared discussions, and other modes.
- Facilitate learning by maintaining a teaching presence, providing reflection tools and instruction in their use, giving regular feedback, and promoting social support and coping strategies.

Points for Reflection
- What other recommendations would you add for colleagues who want to use (more) technology in their TESOL service-learning projects?

CONCLUSION

When John Dewey (1933) spoke about the complexities of reflective thought, he was likely not envisioning the use of today's technology that can bring both benefits and challenges to the process. While technology has been used in various ways to support reflections in service-learning for some time, new platforms and modes of reflection have the potential to transform learning if used strategically. Opportunities to broaden experiences across distances with diverse groups of people, and the effective use of collaborative tools that enable thinking to become visible can enhance learning immensely.

Transitioning from face-to-face service-learning to e-service-learning – whatever the type – provides us with an opportunity to rethink and restructure traditional TESOL service-learning courses in ways that best align goals, outcomes, and objectives with relevant technology.

Chapter 7

Ways Forward in Reflective Practice in TESOL Service-Learning

INTRODUCTION

This chapter considers ways forward in reflective practice in TESOL service-learning. It is a chance to pause and reflect on our existing programs and think about what they could be. I am proud to be in TESOL because, beyond helping preservice ESOL teachers develop the academic knowledge and cognitive and professional skills they need for teaching English to multilingual learners, effective TESOL programs also help individuals develop reflective practice and important social and personal qualities, like cultural awareness, empathy, open-mindedness, collegiality, and more. These are desired university outcomes and important qualities for people who work with diverse populations.

When service-learning experiences are integrated into TESOL programs, all of the desired skills, reflective practice, and character-building qualities can be emphasized and broadened to include a sense of civic responsibility through community engagement. This happens as service-learning raises their awareness of community needs, and helps participants work towards meeting those needs while they strive to meet their academic/cognitive, professional, social/civic, and personal goals. Reflection, a crucial element of service-learning, prompts participants to think about how they can become more effective ESOL teachers and civically minded citizens who seek to improve society by advocating for English learners. Further, critical reflection can help participants to think about ways to effect positive social change, which can truly transform learning.

> **Points for Reflection**
> - Are you convinced of the benefits of reflective practice in TESOL service-learning?

Of course, this is not to say that service-learning and effective reflection will necessarily result in positive social change; indeed, there is no guarantee that even target academic goals will be achieved. Results will depend on quality teaching, strong community relationships, and well-designed service-learning projects. In addition, effective reflection is complex, takes time, and requires frequent practice; hence, one TESOL service-learning experience is typically not sufficient for achieving all goals. Nevertheless, these complexities should not discourage us from implementing a service-learning approach. The hope is that by facilitating effective reflection on the service experience TESOL educators can inspire preservice teachers to develop a culture of reflective practice and community engagement that will help them continue to pursue these goals into the future.

> **Points for Reflection**
> - Where do you see reflective practice in TESOL service-learning going from here? What else can we learn?

Looking ahead, we can consider several ways to move forward. First, we can provide more opportunities for service-learning to be integrated into our TESOL programs. Second, we can work to facilitate more effective reflections in TESOL service-learning. Third, we can encourage more critical reflection in TESOL service-learning contexts. Fourth, we can embrace the positive impacts of technology on reflective practice and on service-learning generally. Finally, we can share more research and stories of reflection in TESOL service-learning to inform future practices and build the evidence needed to gain more support for service-learning in our TESOL programs.

PROVIDING MORE OPPORTUNITIES TO INTEGRATE SERVICE-LEARNING AND EFFECTIVE REFLECTION IN TESOL PROGRAMS

In a 2020 article in *Politico*, Roth commented on the general disconnect between university and community:

> we need the federal government to incentivize more states to create their own programs to integrate education, job training and public service. Colleges and universities can support their states' efforts

to develop programs that incentivize teamwork, innovation, and civic preparedness beyond borders of campus.

Also in 2020, Bok, the former president of Harvard University, advocated greater civic and character education in American universities by envisioning a country in which college graduates "participated in cooperative efforts to improve their communities and welcomed opportunities to join with others to address needs and solve problems, either local, national or global through public service, political activity or membership in nonprofit citizen organizations" (p. 137). A year earlier, in *TESOL Quarterly*, Rose (2019) proposed a dismantling of the ivory tower. While Rose was referring to the separation of TESOL researchers and practitioners, the notion of an ivory tower in TESOL can be perceived as a general isolation of the field from the community. Such calls for universities to strengthen civics and global citizenship education and increase community engagement have been echoed in multiple contexts globally (Aujla & Hamm, 2018; Isaacs et al., 2016; Larsen, 2014; Patrick et al., 2019; Roth & Hohn, 2016; Rusu et al., 2015; Tan & Soo, 2020; Tapia, 2012; Wu, 2015). Indeed, "[r]esearch supports the capacity of well-designed service-learning to enhance many of the humanizing attributes that are included in the Council of Europe's framework for democratic competences (e.g. empathy, self-efficacy, openness to others, cooperation, cultural otherness, civic-mindedness, tolerance of ambiguity)" (Bringle & Clayton, 2020, p. 57). We are reminded that, in some contexts, *civic engagement* is referred to as *solidarity* in order to emphasize the collaborative aspects of service-learning.

Points for Reflection

- Do you agree that community engagement can help dismantle notions of the "ivory tower"?
- Do you think preservice teachers are sufficiently civically minded currently? Can we prepare them more through TESOL service-learning?

Undoubtedly, TESOL practicum helps build connections between a university and local community, and it provides useful experience for helping preservice teachers develop and reflect on their ELT competencies. Often, however, rather than building a community of learners where preservice teachers can learn from each other, the practicum can be an isolating experience limited by the power differential between the supervisor and preservice teacher and, in turn, between the preservice teacher and the ELs. The very term, *supervisor*, emphasizes this imbalance and may result in reflections that are less critical or honest than they could be. There may also be a lack of opportunity and motivation to reflect on community engagement and issues beyond the immediate teaching context. In addition, if the practicum is not conducted carefully, the benefits may seem one-sided, which can potentially – though unintentionally – reinforce deficit mindsets when teaching ELs.

Service-learning in TESOL programs can bring the university and community together to engage in mutually beneficial work using a collaborative approach to teaching and learning. When well implemented, preservice ESOL teachers work together with the community partners and TESOL instructors to achieve the project goals. Importantly, participants are encouraged to reflect together and learn from each other. As discussed in Chapter 2, reflection is a process. It is not a not a one-off task for the purpose of solving problems. Rather, as Rogers (2002) explains, reflection is a way for us to make our experiences meaningful in our lives. Reflection can deepen our understanding, and, through interaction with others, it can open our minds and broaden our perspectives. Results, though perhaps not immediately evident, can help in the development of more civically responsible, empathetic, and culturally and socially aware individuals. With growing evidence of the benefits of service-learning, it is hoped that decision-makers can be persuaded to support more service-learning projects in TESOL programs.

Going forward, it may be possible in some contexts to expand connections between TESOL and multiple community organizations. For example, TESOL service-learning projects might involve both schools and care homes or animal shelters, where preservice teachers might help ELs prepare oral presentations for seniors or interview them and then write their biography, or they might arrange for ELs to read aloud to animals. By emphasizing the contributions of multilingual learners in this way and by reflecting on experiences with them, an asset-based approach could be reinforced, which is another important aspect of community collaboration. TESOL instructors could also arrange service-learning projects with instructors in other disciplines, like education or social work or medicine to meet social or medical needs of communities of people whose English proficiency may prevent them from receiving essential services. Reflective practice in such contexts could be enhanced by discussions with people from other fields who may view events from very different perspectives. Building a community of learners and expanding this community to include other partners in this way has the potential to increase learning. While there may be logistical and other challenges, once partnerships are set up, ongoing cycles can be established to make them sustainable.

Points for Reflection
- Can you envision a service-learning project that involves multiple organizations or disciplines?
- How might the reflective practice be expanded to include these other groups?

FACILITATING MORE EFFECTIVE REFLECTIONS

Research on reflective practice in service-learning (Ash & Clayton, 2005; Barnes & Caprino, 2016; Bradley, 1995; Eyler, 2002a; Jacoby, 2014) supports my own experience that without guidance most students do not always reflect in ways that meet instructor expectations. For example, rather than reflecting on causes of behaviors observed in service-learning experiences or considering alternatives, many preservice teachers simply describe events or feelings. While descriptions and emotions are important, reflections can be expanded to include more meaningful learning points. Chapter 4 presents tools and strategies to do this. To recap, we can motivate preservice ESOL teachers to reflect more deeply by:

- communicating expectations in a transparent way
- explicitly teaching the reflection process and providing selected models of the process that best meet needs
- monitoring comprehension, acknowledging uncertainties and frustrations, and encouraging questions
- presenting examples of meaningful reflections in various formats
- providing tools and clear prompts for reflection
- establishing frequent opportunities for reflection discussions
- allowing choices of reflection platform within required parameters
- monitoring reflections and giving feedback.

The more that instructors provide effective guidance, support, opportunity, encouragement, and feedback, the more they demonstrate that reflective practice is valued. The more that preservice teachers engage in reflective practice and see the benefits for their learning, the greater the potential that they will value reflective practice. The more that reflective practice is valued, the greater chance there is that it might become normalized so that, as we move forward, a culture of reflective practice can emerge and continue into future practice. Realistically, not all individuals will develop strong skills in reflective practice in one service-learning course or program and there are clear challenges in fostering effective reflective practice, but we should not be discouraged. People learn at their own pace and many simply need more time and practice to develop.

We also should not reduce reflective practice to one prescribed model or set of principles to follow in a mechanistic or robotic manner, as Farrell (2019) reminds us. In service-learning, we therefore need to consider the context and customize reflection tasks to the purpose and objectives. Ultimately, reflective practice should help participants make meaning and learn from their experience in a way that strengthens community, builds civic responsibility, promotes participants' development, and informs their current and future practice.

> **Points for Reflection**
> - Knowing that there are no guarantees that learning will improve through reflective practice, is it worth your time and effort to help preservice teachers engage in effective reflective practice?

ENCOURAGING CRITICAL REFLECTION IN TESOL SERVICE-LEARNING CONTEXTS

TESOL celebrates diversity because sharing ideas, languages, and cultures broadens minds, builds community, and drives innovation and creativity (TESOL, 2020). Celebrating diversity and building community are particularly important as local and global problems and issues, like xenophobia, stereotyping, discrimination, inequalities, and race crime continue to remind us that there is much work to be done to improve our world. Schneider (2019) asserts that we need to move beyond traditional TESOL programs to raise awareness of social justice issues related to language education. He claims that

> [c]ommunity-based service-learning offers a unique method for helping
> TESOL students see language learners in relation to the larger social
> world. Furthermore, it allows emerging teachers to recognize that their
> own identities exist in relation to the larger social world (p. 3).

I support this view and note the importance of critical reflection in this process. Jacoby (2014) strenuously advocates the kind of critical reflection in service-learning that raises awareness of the causes of social injustices and generates ideas for working towards positive social change. Similarly, Gorski and Dalton (2020) echo this support for critical reflection in service-learning as it "enhances not only our abilities to explore our own experiences and ideologies but also our abilities to understand our positionalities relative to injustice and responsibilities to eliminate injustice" (pp. 365–366).

The benefits notwithstanding, critical reflection can be challenging and, as discussed in Chapter 2, research shows that it is typically the least likely type of reflection to emerge. There are, however, a number of actions TESOL instructors can take to help foster critical reflection. Instructors can start by introducing relevant texts that explore issues of identity and social justice. They can provide explicit instruction on how to "see language learners (and their own positionality) in relation to the larger social world", as Schneider (2019) suggests, and encourage ESOL preservice teachers to question norms and challenge assumptions and beliefs. They can provide opportunities for critical discussion and other activities, and they can model what critical reflection might look like. Fostering critical reflection needs to be done mindfully because there can be risks when individuals feel pushed to reflect on issues outside their comfort zones and critical reflection may sometimes lead to rumination and unhealthy feelings. To address such concerns, instructors need to establish a safe, non-judgmental environment that fuels hope for positive change while grappling with difficult issues. They need to acknowledge feelings, offer guidance and support for the process of critical reflection, continually monitor reflections, and provide responsive feedback.

It is noted that critical reflection may not be suitable in all contexts for various reasons and instructors need to select approaches that best meet the needs of their contexts. Contexts can change, however, so critical reflection could be a goal that we continue to strive for in TESOL service-learning.

Points for Reflection

- How likely are you to promote critical reflection in TESOL service-learning contexts?

EMBRACING THE POSITIVE IMPACTS OF TECHNOLOGY

A decade ago, Waldner et al. (2012) claimed that "[t]o remain relevant, service-learning must also go online" (p. 123). Their argument was that e-service-learning removes geographical barriers to learning and provides online tools that can promote reflection and engagement. Janke (2019), more recently, agrees, pointing out that "Across the globe, we have new, technology-assisted ways to form communities among people who will never meet in person, but who feel attachment and affiliation as new ways are discovered to organize geographically disparate individuals into unified, collective, and booming voices" (pp. 240–241). Certainly, technology can add possibilities where otherwise there might not have been an opportunity for service-learning. In my own experience, the COVID-19 pandemic meant in-person visits to community sites were not possible, so, over Zoom with our community partner, we re-examined the needs and reconceptualized the TESOL service-learning project from a face-to-face after-school program for ELs to a digital materials development project. Groups of preservice teachers worked together to create themed units with short language activities presented on video and supported by worksheets that the learners could do at home or during scheduled autonomous learning time. The preservice teachers reflected together on the process and other issues orally on Zoom, in written collaborations on Google Docs, individually in journals, and on final assignments. As discussed in Chapter 6, e-service-learning can motivate participants to be more forthcoming in their reflections and potentially build larger communities for collaborative reflection through web-based journaling and multimodal presentations. I am hoping that, in future cohorts, it may be possible for the preservice teachers in my TESOL course to work over Zoom to help the ELs create their own videos, which would clearly demonstrate an asset-based orientation. Reflections on this process might be enhanced by integrating the voices of the multilingual learners as they themselves reflect on what they learned in the process

Going forward, we should seek ways to use technology in TESOL service-learning when it means greater participation and inclusion and benefits reflective practice, but we shouldn't get distracted by the technology. We need to be reminded that, like in traditional formats of service-learning, reflective practice in e-service-learning can be successful when clear communication of expectations with modeling is provided and training is included for all participants including instructor, participants, and community partners. In addition, technological challenges, like incompatible hardware and/or software need to be addressed in advance. Bringle and Clayton (2020) advise that high-quality integration of service-learning and digital technology must draw on best practices of each, including alignment of learning objectives, assessment, engagement of learners, course technology, and desired outcomes. Guthrie and McCracken (2014) claim that e-service-learning can provide rich opportunities for reflection and learning, stating, "[e]-service-learning courses enable increasingly personal learning through customizable technologies, individual experiences, and collective spaces that combine to produce emergent meaning: a new direction for teaching, learning, and reflecting" (p. 250). Like Bringle and Clayton (2020), Guthrie and McCracken (2014) caution that reflection must be a guided process, aligned with institutional goals. They add that interactive reflections and discussions may be less effective in large class sizes if participants are reluctant to share emotional stories. We should be aware, too, that face-to-face service-learning continues to be preferred, or required, in many contexts.

As technological tools used in reflective practice evolve, and research on e-service-learning increases, our understanding of its value and related issues will continue to grow.

Points for Reflection
- How would you convince a colleague that reflective practice in service-learning might be enhanced with technology?

SHARING MORE RESEARCH AND STORIES OF REFLECTION IN TESOL SERVICE-LEARNING

The large number of journals, books, scholarly papers, conferences, organizations, web resources, learning networks, and communities on the subject of service-learning is evidence of the high value that people and institutions globally place on this approach to teaching and learning. That said, the focus on reflection, particularly in TESOL service-learning contexts, is much less extensive, so more attention is needed in this area. More work is also needed on reflection by community partners so that this important perspective can be heard. Reflection is what makes the service-learning experience meaningful, so we need to continue researching, talking about, and sharing our experiences in this area so that we can learn from one another and use that knowledge to inform and advance reflective practice in TESOL service-learning.

We need to continue making strides in demonstrating how reflections on TESOL service-learning can provide evidence of learning and the achievement of outcomes. Work in e-service-learning and the use of technology in the reflection process can be discussed and shared to help others make informed decisions about how they can best use technology to support reflective practice in other contexts. Less traditional forms of reflection, such as performance, artwork, and community action can be studied to determine how they demonstrate evidence of the reflective process. What interests me personally is learning about what others are doing to facilitate critical reflection in TESOL service-learning and the impacts that has.

The more evidence there is in the form of published research on the benefits of TESOL service-learning and reflective practice, the more we learn and the more persuasive our argument can be for adopting this approach.

Points for Reflection
- Do you have ideas for facilitating reflective practice in a TESOL service-learning project that you could share?
- What do you think the focus of future research should be so that it could inform reflective practice in this context?

CONCLUSION

TESOL service-learning is growing in importance as a learning approach that promotes community engagement while addressing both academic and community needs. It can strengthen community, promote the development of positive human qualities, increase the sense of civic responsibility, and help raise awareness of social justice issues. This is particularly relevant in TESOL, as global events demonstrate that culturally and linguistically diverse people often face unfair disadvantages and need advocates.

As an essential part of the service-learning experience, reflection can deepen understandings of TESOL course content and its practical applications. The process of reflection can impel participants to grapple with the complexities of their experiences, and, through interaction and reflection with others, it can open their minds and broaden perspectives, enabling them to rethink and build on their knowledge, skills, beliefs, attitudes, and civic responsibilities.

There is still work to be done on critical reflection in TESOL service-learning. We can try to help preservice teachers reflect on their own identities, values, assumptions, and positionalities in interactions with others. We can help them to view learners in broader contexts and raise awareness of social injustices. When preservice teachers are prompted to rethink their beliefs and reach new understandings of themselves and the community, they are transforming their learning and contributing to social good.

After reading the chapters in this book, readers should have a better understanding of the value of service-learning and the importance and complexities of reflective practice in a TESOL service-learning context. It is hoped that the discussion and practical tools for fostering effective reflection in TESOL service-learning provide some insight into what reflection in TESOL service-learning might look like, as well as inspire readers to consider these and other ideas for implementing reflective practice in other TESOL service-learning contexts.

References

Al Akhawayn University Office of Community Engagement (n.d.). http://www.aui.ma/en/CommunityInvolvement

Albanesi, C., Culcasi, I., & Zunszain, P. (Eds) (n.d.). *Practical guide on e-service-learning in response to COVID-19*. European Observatory of Service-Learning in Higher Education. https://www.eoslhe.eu/easlhe/

Asghar, M., & Rowe, N. (2017). Reciprocity and critical reflection as the key to social justice in service-learning: A case study. *Innovation in Education and Teaching International*, *54*(2), 117–125. http://dx.doi.org/10.1080/14703297.2016.1273788

Ash, S. L., & Clayton, P. H. (2004). The articulated learning: An approach to guided reflection and assessment. *Innovative Higher Education*, *29*(2), 137–154.

Ash, S. L., & Clayton, P. H. (2009). Generating, deepening, and documenting learning: The power of critical reflection in applied learning. *Journal of Applied Learning in Higher Education*, *1*, 25–48.

Ash, S. L., Clayton, P. H., & Atkinson, M. P. (2005). Integrating reflection and assessment to capture and improve student learning. *Michigan Journal of Community Service Learning*, *11*(2), 49–60.

Association of International Schools in Africa (AISA) (2016). *Handbook for service-learning*. https://aoisia49.wildapricot.org/resources/Documents/Service%20Learning/AISA%20Service%20Learning%20Resources/AISA%20Service%20Learning%20Handbook%202016%20FINAL%20(10May2016).pdf

Atkinson Smolen, L., Zhang, W., & Detwiler, S. (2013). Engaged teaching and learning with adult Karen refugees in a service-learning site. *TESOL Journal*, *4*(3), 534–554. DOI: 10.1002/tesj.94

Aujla, W., & Hamm, Z. (2018). Establishing the roots of community service-learning in Canada: Advocating for a community first approach. *Community Service-Learning in Canada: Emerging Conversations*, *4*(1), 19–37.

Au Yeung, S. N. C., Lam, L. K., & Fong, J. (2019) How service-learning promotes intergenerational harmony: A case study of a service-learning project in a science course. *Metropolitan Universities Journal*, *30*(3), 20–35.

Averett, P. E., & Arnd-Caddigan, M. (2014). Preparing BSW students for service-learning: Enhancing epistemological reflection. *Journal of Teaching in Social Work, 34*, 316–331. DOI: 10.1080/08841233.2014.907222

Barnes, M. E., & Caprino, K. (2016). Analyzing service-learning reflections through Fink's taxonomy. *Teaching in Higher Education, 21*(5), 557–575, DOI: 10.1080/13562517.2016.1160221

Becker, S., & Paul, C. (2015). "It didn't seem like race mattered": Exploring the implications of service-learning pedagogy for reproducing or challenging color blind racism. *Teaching Sociology, 43*(3), 184–200. DOI: 10.1177/0092055X15587987

Becker, S., Lima, M., Baumgartner, J., Babcock, G., & Forrest, D. (2020). *E-service-learning: Best practices, pitfalls to avoid, and recommendations*. LSU Center for Community Engagement, Learning and Leadership. https://www.lsu.edu/academicaffairs/ccell/eservice-learning_report.pdf

Birdwell, J., Scott, R., & Horley, E. (2013). Active citizenship, education and service learning. *Education, Citizenship and Social Justice, 8*(2), 185–199. DOI: 10.1177/1746197913483683

Bloom, B. S. (1956). *Taxonomy of educational objectives, Handbook I: The cognitive domain*. David McKay Co. Inc.

Bok, D. (2020). *Higher expectations: Can colleges teach students what they need to know in the 21st century?* Princeton University Press.

Bolger, M. (2018, February 16). Why I don't facilitate privilege walks anymore and what I do instead. *Medium*. https://medium.com/@MegB/why-i-dont-won-t-facilitate-privilege-walks-anymore-and-what-i-do-instead-380c95490e10

Bolger, M. (n.d.). *Privilege for sale*. Social Justice Toolbox. https://www.socialjusticetoolbox.com/activity/privilege-for-sale/

Bouffard, L. (2020, June 18). 5 reasons police officers should have college degrees. *The Conversation*. https://theconversation.com/5-reasons-police-officers-should-have-college-degrees-140523

Bradley, J. (1995). A model for evaluating student learning in academically based service. In M. Troppe (Ed.), *Connecting cognition and action: Evaluation of student performance in service-learning courses* (pp. 13–27). Campus Compact.

Brail, S. (2016). Quantifying the value of service-learning: A comparison of grade achievement between service-learning and non-service-learning students. *International Journal of Teaching and Learning in Higher Education, 28*(2), 148–157.

Bringle, R. G., & Clayton, P. H. (2012). Civic education through service learning: What, how, and why? In L. McIlrath, A. Lyons, & R. Munck (Eds), *Higher Education and Civic Engagement* (pp. 101–124). Palgrave Macmillan.

Bringle, R. G., & Clayton, P. H. (2020). Integrating service learning and digital technologies: Examining the challenge and the promise. *RIED. Revista Iberoamericana de Educación a Distancia, 23*(1), 43–65. doi: http://dx.doi.org/10.5944/ried.23.1.25386

Bringle, R. G., & Hatcher, J. A. (1999). Reflection in service-learning: Making meaning or experience. *Evaluation/Reflection, 23*. https://digitalcommons.unomaha.edu/slceeval/23

Brookfield, S. D. (1995). *Becoming a critically reflective teacher*. Jossey-Bass.

Brown University Library (n.d.). *The Education Alliance at Brown University collection*. Brown Digital Repository. https://repository.library.brown.edu/studio/collections/1041/

Burke, A. M., Case, S., & Hamstra, C. (2021). TESOL service learning program in rural Michigan: An innovative approach to preparing pre-service teachers. *MITEOL Journal*, *3*(1), 1–34.

Busch, B. (2010). School language profiles: Valorizing linguistic resources in heteroglossic situations in South Africa. *Language and Education*, *24*(4), 283–294. https://doi-org.ezproxy.emich.edu/10.1080/09500781003678712

Butin, D. (2011). Service-learning as an intellectual movement. In T. Stewart, & N. Webster (Eds), *Problematizing service-learning: Critical reflections for development and action* (pp. 19–35). Information Age Publishing, Inc.

Calvert, V., & Valladares Montemayor, H. (2018). Community service-learning: Why can't Canada be more like Mexico? *Engaged Scholar Journal*, *4*(1), 39–57.

Carney, T. M. (2004). Reaching beyond borders through service learning. *Journal of Latinos & Education*, *3*(4), 267–271.

Carrington, S., & Selva, G. (2010). Critical social theory and transformative learning: Evidence in pre-service teachers' service-learning reflection logs. *Higher Education Research & Development*, *29*(1), 45–57. DOI: 10.1080/07294360903421384

Celio, C. I., Durlak, D., & Dymnicki, A. (2011). A meta-analysis of the impact of service-learning on students. *Journal of Experiential Education*, *34*(2), 164–181.

Chambers, T. (2009). A continuum of service-learning approaches within Canadian post-secondary education. *Canadian Journal of Higher Education*, *39*(2), 77–100.

Cho, H., & Gulley, J. (2017). A catalyst for change: Service-learning for TESOL graduate students. *TESOL Journal*, *8*(3), 613–635. DOI: 10.1002/tesj.289

Coulson, D., & Harvey, M. (2013). Scaffolding student reflection for experience-based learning: A framework. *Teaching in Higher Education*, *18*(4), 401–413.

Council of Europe (2018). *Reference framework of competencies for democratic culture,* volumes 1, 2, and 3. Strasbourg Cedex. https://www.coe.int/en/web/reference-framework-of-competences-for-democratic-culture/rfcdc-volumes

Cramer, J., & Toso, B. W. (2015). *Family service learning brief*. National Center for Families Learning. https://www.familieslearning.org/pdf/NCFL-FSL-brief_F3.pdf

Crosby, C. R. (2017). Benefits of community engagement in an online TESOL course for teachers in globalized spaces. In C. R. Crosby & F. Brockmeier (Eds), *Community engagement program implementation and teacher preparation for 21st century education* (pp. 172–183). IGI Global.

Dailey-Hebert, A., & Donnelli-Sallee, E. (2010). Service-elearning: Educating today's learners for an unscripted future. *International Journal of Organizational Analysis*, *18*(2), 216–227. DOI: 10.1108/19348831011046272

Dailey-Hebert, A. Donnelli-Sallee, E., & DiPadova-Stocks, L. N. (Eds) (2008). *Service-elearning: Educating for citizenship*. Information Age Publishing.

Delano-Oriaran, O., Penick-Parks, M. W., & Fondrie, S. (2015). *The SAGE sourcebook of service-learning and civic engagement*. Sage Publications.

Dewey, J. (1910). *How we think.* D. C. Heath & Co.

Dewey, J. (1916). *Democracy and education.* Echo Library edition, Macmillan, 2007.

Dewey, J. (1933). *How we think: A restatement of the relation of reflective thinking to the educative process.* Houghton Mifflin.

Dewey, J. (1938). *Experience and education.* Kappa Delta Phi.

Diversi, M., & Mecham, C. (2005). Latino(a) students and Caucasian mentors in a rural after-school program: Towards empowering adult–youth relationships. *Journal of Community Psychology, 33*(1), 31–40.

Dubinsky, J. M., Welch, M., & Wurr, A. J. (2012). Composing cognition: The role of written reflections in service-learning. In I. Baca (Ed.), *Service-learning and writing: Paving the way for literacy(ies) through community engagement* (pp. 155–180). Brill.

Early, J., & Lasker, G. A. (2018). Strengthening communities of inquiry online and offline: Exploring the benefits and challenges of including service-learning in a fully online women's global health course. *Pedagogy in Health Promotion: The Scholarship of Teaching and Learning, 4*(3), 218–226. DOI: 10.1177/2373379917730843

Echevarría, J., Vogt, M. E., & Short, D. (2017). *Making content comprehensible for English language learners: The SIOP model* (5th Ed.). Allyn & Bacon.

Elon University's Center for Engaged Learning (n.d.). https://www.centerforengagedlearning. org/doing-engaged-learning/service-learning/

Epstein, S. E. (2011). Who's in charge? Examining the complex nature of student voice in service-learning projects. In T. Stewart & N. Webster (Eds), *Problematizing service-learning: Critical reflections for development and action* (pp. 175–200). Information Age Publishing, Inc.

Ericsson, K. A., & Simon, H. A. (1993). *Protocol analysis: Verbal reports as data.* MIT Press.

European Observatory of Service-Learning in Higher Education (n.d.). *What we do. Service-learning.* https://www.eoslhe.eu/what-we-do/

Eyler, J. (2000). What do we most need to know about the impact of service-learning on student learning? *Michigan Journal of Community Service Learning, Special Issue, 1,* 11–17.

Eyler, J. (2002a). Reflection: Linking service and learning. *Journal of Social Issues, 58*(3), 517–534.

Eyler, J. (2002b). Reflecting on service: Helping nursing students get the most from service-learning. *Journal of Nursing Education, 41*(10), 453–456.

Eyler, J., Giles Jr., D. E., & Schmiede, A. (1996). *A practitioner's guide to reflection in service-learning: Student voices and reflections.* Vanderbilt University.

Facing History and Ourselves (n.d.). *Teaching strategies: Identity charts.* https://www. facinghistory.org/resource-library/teaching-strategies/identity-charts

Fairbairn, S., & Jones-Vo, S. (2010). *Differentiating instruction and assessment for English language learners: A guide for K-12 teachers.* Calson Publishing.

Farrell, T. S. C. (2015). *Promoting teacher reflection in second language education: A framework for TESOL professionals.* Routledge.

Farrell, T. S. C. (2019). *Reflective practice in ELT.* Equinox Publishing.

Felten, P., & Clayton, P. H. (2011). Service-learning. *New Directions for Teaching and Learning, 128* (Special Edition: Evidence-based Teaching), 75–84. doi: 10.1002/Tl

Fink, L. D. (2013). *Creating significant learning outcomes: An integrated approach to designing college courses.* Jossey-Bass.

Fitts, S., & Gross, L. A. (2012). Teacher candidates learning from English learners: Constructing concepts of language and culture in Tuesday's Tutors after-school program. *Teacher Education Quarterly, 39*(4), 75–95.

Folgueiras, P., Villa, R., & Aneas, A. (2019). What factors promote participation at school among adolescents in secondary education? *Revista de cercetare și intervenție socială, 66,* 364–377.

Foste, Z. (2018). Exploring the methodological possibilities of narrative inquiry in service-learning: Reflections from a recent investigation. *Journal of Higher Education Outreach and Engagement, 22*(4), 9–28.

Furco, A., Root, S., & Furco, A. (2010). Research demonstrates the value of service learning. *Phi Delta Kappan, 91*(5), 16–20.

Garrison, D. R., & Kanuka, H. (2004). Blended learning: Uncovering its transformative potential in higher education. *Internet and Higher Education, 7,* 95–105.

Garrison, D. R., Anderson, T., & Archer, W. (2010). The first decade of the community of inquiry framework: A retrospective. *Internet and Higher Education, 13,* 5–9.

Garver, R. A., Eslami, Z. R., & Tong, F. (2018). I believe I can: Service-learning to raise preservice teacher's efficacy with English learners. *The Reading Matrix, 18*(2), 23–37.

Gasper-Hulvat, M. (2018). "More like a real human being": Humanizing historical artists through remote service-learning. *Journal of Experiential Education, 41*(4), 397–410. DOI: 10.1177/1053825918808321

Gee, J. P. (2005). *An introduction to discourse analysis: Theory and method.* Routledge.

Gelmon, S. B., Holland, B. A., & Spring, A. (2018). *Assessing service-learning and civic engagement: Principles and techniques.* Stylus Publishing.

Giles, D. E. (2019). The emergence of engaged scholarship: Seven additional years of evolution. In L. Sandmann & D. Jones (Eds), *Building the field of higher education engagement foundational ideas and future directions* (pp. 171–174). Stylus Publishing.

Goh, K. C., D'Rozario, V., Ch'ng, T. H. A., & Cheah, H. M. (2009). *Character development through service and experiential learning.* Pearson Education.

Gorski, P. C., & Dalton, K. (2020). Striving for critical reflection in multicultural and social justice teacher education: Introducing a typology of reflection approaches. *Journal of Teacher Education, 71*(3), 357–368. https://doi.org/10.1177/0022487119883545

Gottlieb, K., & Robinson, G. (Eds) (2006). *A practical guide for integrating civic responsibility into the curriculum.* Community College Press.

Grekul, J., Aujla, W., Eklics, G., Manca, T., York, A. E., & Aylsworth, L. (2018). Community service-learning in a large introductory sociology course: Reflections on the instructional experience. *Engaged Scholar Journal, 4*(1), 61–78.

Grönlund, H., Nortomaa, A., Aramburuzabala, P., McIlrath, L., Opazo, H., Altenburger, R., Maas, S., Mažeikiene, N. Meijs, L. C. P. M., Mikelic, N., Millican, J., Stark, J., Tuytschaever, G., Vargas-Moniz, M., & Zani, B. (2017). *Guidelines for institutionalization of service-learning*. Europe Engage. https://europeengage.org/9-guidelines-and-recommendations-for-institutionalization-of-s-l-in-higher-education/

Guthrie, K. L., & McCracken, H. (2014). Reflection: The importance of making meaning in e-service-learning courses. *Journal of Computing in Higher Education, 26*, 238–252. DOI: 10.1007/s12528-014-9087-9

Harris, U. S. (2017). Virtual partnerships: Engaging students in e-service learning using computer-mediated communication. *Asia Pacific Media Educator, 27*(1), 103–117. DOI: 10.1177/1326365X17701792

Hatcher, J. A., & Bringle, R. G. (1997) Reflection: Bridging the gap between service and learning. *College Teaching, 45*(4), 153–158. DOI: 10.1080/87567559709596221

Hatcher, J. A., Bringle, R. G., & Muthiah, R. (2004). Designing effective reflection: What matters to service-learning? *Michigan Journal of Community Service Learning, 11*(1), 38–46.

Hatton, N., & Smith, D. (1995). Reflection in teacher education: Towards definition and implementation. *Teaching and Teacher Education, 11*(1), 33–49.

Hicks, Q., Hammond, B. M., Winters, R. L., & Boersma, J. (2019). Identifying the influence of factors on the quality of critical reflection: Framing, frequency, and feedback. *Journal of Applied Learning and Teaching, 2*(1), 7–15. https://journals.sfu.ca/jalt/index.php/jalt/article/view/55/51

Hickson, H. (2020). Learning how to be reflective. In L. Béres, & J. Fook (Eds), *Learning critical reflection: Experiences of the transformative learning process* (pp. 55–65). Routledge.

Hill-Jackson, V., & Lewis, C. W. (2011). In T. Stewart, & N. Webster (Eds), *Problematizing service-learning: Critical reflections for development and action* (pp. 295–321). Information Age Publishing.

Hullender, R., Hinck, S., Wood-Nartker, J., Burton, T., & Bowlby, S. (2015). Evidences of transformative learning in service-learning reflections. *Journal of the Scholarship of Teaching and Learning, 15*(4), 58–82. DOI: 10.14434/josotl.v15i4.13432

Huxley, A. (1933). *Texts and pretexts: An anthology with commentaries*. Harper & Brothers Publishers.

Isaacs, S., Rose, J., & Davids, C. (2016). Transformative learning: Postgraduate students' reflections on a community engagement program in South Africa. *Social Behavior and Personality, 44*(1), 103–116. http://dx.doi.org/10.2224/sbp.2016.44.1.103

Jacoby, B. (2014). *Service-learning essentials: Questions, answers, and lessons learned.* Jossey-Bass.

Jaeger, E. L. (2013). Teacher reflection: Supports, barriers, and results. *Issues in Teacher Education, 22*(1), 89–104.

Janke, E. M. (2019). Next-generation scholars and scholarly communications. In L. Sandmann & D. Jones (Eds), *Building the field of higher education engagement foundational ideas and future directions* (pp. 240–242). Stylus Publishing.

Jerome, L. (2011). Service learning and active citizenship education in England. *Education, Citizenship and Social Justice, 7*(1) 59–70. DOI: 10.1177/1746197911432594

Kahlke, R., & Taylor, A. (2018). Community service-learning in Canada: One size does not fit all. *Engaged Scholar Journal, 4*(1), 1–18.

Kajder, S. B., & Parkes, K. A. (2012). Examining preservice teachers' reflective practice within and across multimodal writing environments. *Journal of Technology and Teacher Education, 20*(3), 229–249.

Kassabgy, N., & Salah El-Din, Y. (2013). Investigating the impacts of an experiential service-learning course. *TESOL Journal, 4*(3), 571–586. DOI: 10.1002/tesj.92

Kiely, R. (2005). A transformative learning model for service-learning: A longitudinal case study. *Michigan Journal of Community Service Learning, 12*(1), 5–22. http://hdl.handle.net/2027/spo.3239521.0012.101

King, P. M., & Kitchener, K. S. (2004). Reflective judgment: Theory and research on the development of epistemic assumptions through adulthood. *Educational Psychologist, 39*(1), 5–18.

Kolb, D. A. (1984). *Experiential learning: Experience as the source of learning and development.* Prentice-Hall.

Lahav, O., Daniely, N., & Yalon-Chamovitz, S. (2018). Interpersonal social responsibility model of service learning: A longitudinal study. *Scandinavian Journal of Occupational Therapy, 25*(1), 61–69.

Larsen, M. (2014). Critical global citizenship and international service learning: A case study of the intensification effect. *Journal of Global Citizenship & Equity Education, 4*(1), 1–43. https://journals.sfu.ca/jgcee/index.php/jgcee/article/view/112

Leijen, A., Valtna, K., Leijen, D. A. J., & Pedaste, M. (2012). How to determine the quality of students' reflections? *Studies in Higher Education, 37*(2), 203–217.

Lu, C. H., Chen, Z. Y., & Yang, Z. Y. (2019) Introductory service-learning experience: Macau college students in ethnic minority school of mountain area in China. *Metropolitan Universities Journal, 30*(3), 10–19.

Ma, H. K. C., Chiu, T., & Lim, T. W. (2019). Service-learning in Asia. *Metropolitan Universities Journal, 30*(3), 3–9.

Macknish, C., Tomaš, Z., & Vojtkulakova, M. (2018). Examining performance and attitudes of TESOL preservice teachers and their English learners in a service-learning project. *The Reading Matrix, 18*(2) 3–22. http://www.readingmatrix.com/files/19-45a952bw.pdf

Maddux, H.C., & Donnett, D. (2015). John Dewey's pragmatism: Implications for reflection in service-learning. *Michigan Journal of Community Service Learning, 21*(2), 64–73.

Martin, F., & Pirbhai-Illich, F. (2015). Service-learning as post-colonial discourse: Active global citizenship. In R. Reynolds, D. Bradbery, J. Brown, K. Carroll, D. Donnelly, K. Ferguson-Patrick, & S. Macqueen. *Contesting and constructing international perspectives in global education* (pp. 135–150). Sense Publishers.

McDonald, B. (2012, October 17). Assessment in service-learning. Non-journal publication. https://files.eric.ed.gov/fulltext/ED535897.pdf

McGowan, V. F. (2017). An assessment of service learning objectives and outcomes. *Journal of Transformative Learning, (4)*2, 43–55.

McIlrath, L., Aramburuzabala, P., Opazo, H., Hopia, A., & Grönlund, H. (2016). *Europe Engage survey of civic engagement and service-learning activities within the partner universities.* Europe Engage Erasmus+project (European Union).

McMillan, J., & Stanton, T. K. (2014). "Learning service" in international contexts: Partnership-based service-learning and research in Cape Town, South Africa. *Michigan Journal of Community Service Learning, 21*(1), 64–78.

Mezirow, J. (2000). *Transformative dimensions of adult learning.* Jossey-Bass.

Molee, L. M., Henry, M. E., Sessa, V. I., & McKinney-Prupis, E. R. (2010). Assessing learning in service-learning courses through critical reflection. *Journal of Experiential Education, 33*(3), 239–257. DOI: 10.5193/JEE33.3.239

Moon, J. (2001). *PDP working paper 4: Reflection in higher education learning.* Generic Center Learning and Teaching Support Network, 1–25. https://nursing-midwifery.tcd.ie/assets/director-staff-edu-dev/pdf/PD-%20Working-Paper-4-Moon.pdf

Mukuria, V. (2008). Civic engagement in Kenya: Developing student leadership through service learning. Unpublished dissertation, Ohio State University.

Murtiningsih, S. R. (2015). Reframing service-learning in curriculum reform in TESOL teacher education in Indonesia. In J. M. Perren & A. J. Wurr (Eds), *Learning the language of global citizenship: Strengthening service-learning in TESOL* (pp. 523–540). Common Ground Publishing.

National Youth Leadership Council (NYLC) (n.d.). Who we are. https://www.nylc.org/page/who-we-are

National Youth Leadership Council (NYLC) (2007). *Teacher tools.* NYLC Resource Center. www.nylc.org

National Youth Leadership Council (NYLC) (2008). *K-12 service-learning standards for quality practice.* https://cdn.ymaws.com/www.nylc.org/resource/resmgr/resources/lift/standards_document_mar2015up.pdf

Newby, D., Allan, R., Fenner, A. B., Jones, B. Komorowska, H., & Soghikyan, K. (2007). *European portfolio for student teachers of languages: A reflection tool for language teacher education.* Council of Europe. https://www.ecml.at/Portals/1/documents/ECML-resources/EPOSTL-EN.pdf?ver=2018-03-22-164301-450

Newman, J. L., Dantzler, J., & Coleman, A. N. (2015). Science in action: How middle school students are changing their world through STEM service-learning projects. *Theory into Practice, 54*(1), 47–54. DOI: 10.1080/00405841.2015.977661

Ngee Ann Polytechnic Office of Service-Learning (n.d.). https://www.np.edu.sg/student-life/service-learning

Nieto, S. (2018). *Language, culture, and teaching: Critical perspectives* (3rd Ed.). Routledge.

Opazo, H., Aramburuzabala, P., & Cerrillo, R. (2016). A review of the situation of service-learning in higher education in Spain. *Asia-Pacific Journal of Cooperative Education, 17*(1), 75–91.

Palpacuer Lee, C., Curtis, J. H., & Curran, M. E. (2018). Shaping the vision for service-learning in language education. *Foreign Language Annals. 51,* 169–184. DOI: 10.1111/flan.12329.

Patrick, C. J., Valencia-Forrester, F., Backhaus, B., McGregor, R., Cain, G., & Lloyd, K. (2019). The state of service-learning in Australia. *Journal of Higher Education Outreach and Engagement, 23*(3), 185–198.

Paul, R., & Elder, L. (2001). *The miniature guide to critical thinking: Concepts and tools.* Foundation for Critical Thinking.

Pawan, F., Wiechart, K. A., Warren, A. N., & Park J. (2016). *Pedagogy and practice for online English language teacher education.* TESOL Press.

Perren, J. M., & Wurr, A. J. (Eds) (2015). *Learning the language of global citizenship: Strengthening service-learning in TESOL.* Common Ground Publishing.

Pipe, L. M., & Stephens, J. T. (2021). Toward a liberated learning spirit: A model for developing critical consciousness. *Journal of the Scholarship of Teaching and Learning, 21*(2), 121–139. doi: 10.14434/josotl.v21i2.29148

Pirbhai-Illich, F. (2013). Crossing borders: At the nexus of critical service-learning, literacy, and social justice. *Waikato Journal of Education, 18*(2), 79–96.

Purmensky, K. L. (2009*). Service-learning for diverse communities: Critical pedagogy and mentoring English language learners.* Information Age Publishing.

Purmensky, K. L. (2015). Bridging the gap for English learners: Service-learning digital mentorship for school success. In J. M. Perren & A. J. Wurr (Eds), *Learning the language of global citizenship: Strengthening service-learning in TESOL*, pp. 569–598. Common Ground Publishing.

Ribeiro A., Aramburuzabala P., & Paz-Lourido B. (Eds) (2021). 2021 *Annual report of European Association of Service-Learning in Higher Education.* Available at: www.euslhe.eu/easlhe

Rodríguez-Izuierdo, R. M. (2021). Does service-learning affect the development of intercultural sensitivity? A study comparing students' progress in two different methodologies. *International Journal of Intercultural Relations, 82,* 99–108.

Rogers, C. (2002). Defining reflection: Another look at John Dewey and reflective thinking. *Teachers College Record, 104*(4), 842–866.

Rose, H. (2019). Dismantling the ivory tower in TESOL: A renewed call for teaching-informed research. *TESOL Quarterly, 53*(3), 895–905. doi: 10.1002/tesq.517

Roth, C., & Hohn, B. (2016). How to interconnect universities with nonprofit organizations for service-learning: A German approach. *International Journal of Research on Service-Learning and Community Engagement, 4*(1), 377–389. http://journals.sfu.ca/iarslce

Roth, M. S. (2020, July 18). Will the pandemic blow up college in America? *Politico.* https://www.politico.com/news/magazine/2020/07/18/will-the-pandemic-blow-up-college-in-america-368067

Ruiz-Ordonez, Y., Salcedo-Mateu, A., Turbi-Pinazo, A. M., Novella-Garcia, C., & Moret-Tatay, C. (2020). CASD-14: A questionnaire on civic attitudes and sustainable development values for service-learning in early adolescents. *Sustainability, 12*(4056). DOI: 10.3390/su12104056

Rusu, A. S., Copaci, I. A., & Soos, A. (2015). The impact of service-learning on improving students' teacher training: Testing the efficiency of a tutoring program in increasing future teachers' civic attitudes, skills and self-efficacy. *Procedia – Social and Behavioral Sciences, 203,* 75–83. DOI: 10.1016/j.sbspro.2015.08.262

Ryan, M. (2012). *Service-learning after learn and serve America: How five states are moving forward*. Education Commission of the States. http://www.ecs.org/clearinghouse/01/02/87/10287.pdf

Salter, P., & Halbert, K. (2019). Balancing classroom ready with community ready: Enabling agency to engage with community through critical service learning. *Asia-Pacific Journal of Teacher Education, 47*(1), 5–17.

Sandaran, S. C. (2012). Service-learning: Transforming students, communities and universities. *Procedia – Social and Behavioral Sciences, 66*, 380–390. DOI: 10.1016/j.sbspro.2012.11.281

Sandy, M. G., & Franco, Z. E. (2014). Grounding service-learning in the digital age: Exploring a virtual sense of geographic place through online collaborative mapping and mixed media. *Journal of Higher Education Outreach and Engagement, 18*(4), 201–232.

Schneider, J. (2019). Teaching in context: Integrating community-based service learning into TESOL education. *TESOL Journal, 10*(1), 1–15. https://doi.org/10.1002/tesj.380

Schön, D. A. (1983). *The reflective practitioner: How professionals think in action*. Basic Books.

Schön, D. A. (1987). *Educating the reflective practitioner*. Jossey-Bass.

Scott, K. E., & Graham, J. A. (2015). Service-learning: Implications for empathy and community engagement in elementary school children. *Journal of Experiential Education, 38*(4), 354–372.

Seilstad, B. (2014). Designing, implementing, and evaluating a department-wide service-learning program for English language learners in Morocco, *Journal of Higher Education Outreach and Engagement, 18*(1), 229–264.

Shapiro, S., Farrelly, R., & Tomaš, Z. (2014). *Fostering international student success in higher education*. TESOL Press.

Smit, E. M., & Tremethick, M. J. (2017). Value of online group reflection after international service-learning experiences: I never thought of that. *Nurse Educator, 42*(6), 286–389.

Smith, B. (2001). Arabic speakers. In M. Swan & B. Smith (Eds), *Learner English: A teacher's guide to interference and other problems* (2nd Ed., pp. 195–213). Cambridge University Press.

Soudy, N., Pessoa, S., & Dias, M. B. (2015). Building bridges through a community English literacy program for low-income migrant workers in Qatar. In J. M. Perren & A. J. Wurr (Eds), *Learning the language of global citizenship: Strengthening service-learning in TESOL* (pp. 358–395). Common Ground Publishing.

Stark, W., Aramburuzabala, P., McIlrath, L, Opazo, H., Altenburger, R., Grönlund, Maas, S., Mažeikiene, Meijs, L. C. P. M., Mikelic, N., Millican, J., Nortomaa, A, Tuytschaever, G., Vargas-Moniz, M., & Zani, B. (2016). *Quality standards for service learning activities*. Europe Engage.

Steinberg, K., Hatcher, J. A., & Bringle, R. G. (2011). A north star: Civic-minded graduate. *Michigan Journal of Community Service Learning, 17*(1), 19–33.

Stefaniak, J. (2020). A systems view of supporting the transfer of learning through e-service-learning experiences in real-world contexts. *Tech Trends, 64*, 561–569. https://doi.org/10.1007/s11528-020-00487-3

Stewart, T. (2011). Opening up service-learning reflection by turning inward: Developing mindful learners through contemplation. In T. Stewart & N. Webster (Eds), *Problematizing service-learning: Critical reflections for development and action* (pp. 37–67). Information Age Publishing.

Stewart, T., & N. Webster (Eds) (2011). *Problematizing service-learning: Critical reflections for development and action.* Information Age Publishing.

Sturgill, A., & Motley, P. (2014). Methods of reflection about service learning: Guided vs. free, dialogic vs. expressive, and public vs. private. *Teaching & Learning Inquiry*, 2(1), 81–93.

Suwaed, H. (2018). The path less taken: Incorporating service-learning in the English language curricula. *IAFOR Journal of Language Learning*, 4(1), 25–40.

Tan, S. Y., & Soo, S. H. J. (2020). Service-learning and the development of student teachers in Singapore. *Asia Pacific Journal of Education*, 40(2), 263–276. DOI: 10.1080/02188791.2019.1671809

Tapia, M. N. (2012). Academic excellence and community engagement: Reflections on the Latin American experience. In L. McIlrath, A. Lyons, & R. Munck (Eds), *Higher education and civic engagement: Comparative perspectives* (pp. 187–203). Palgrave Macmillan.

Tapia Sasot, M. R. (2020). Un itinerario digital para el aprendizaje-servicio ubicuo (A digital itinerary for ubiquitous service-learning). *RIED. Revista Iberoamericana de Educación a Distancia*, 23(1), 111–128. DOI: 10.5944/ried.23.1.25389

Tauscher Birdsall, J. A. (n.d.). *Community voice: Community partners reflect on service learning*, Community & Civic Engagement, Mesa Community College Website https://www.mesacc.edu/community-civic-engagement/journals/community-voice-community-partners-reflect-service-learning

Taylor, A., Butterwick, S., Raykov, M., Glick, S., Peikazadi, N., & Mehrabi, S. (2015). *Community service-learning in Canadian higher education.* UBC Faculty Research and Publications. http://dx.doi.org/10.14288/1.0226035

Terry, A. W., & Bohnenberger, J. E. (2004). Blueprint for incorporating service-learning: A basic, developmental K-12 service-learning typology. *Journal of Experimental Education*, 27(1), 15–31.

TESOL International Association (TESOL) (2018). *Standards for initial TESOL pre-K-12 teacher preparation programs.* TESOL. www.tesol.org/teacher-prep-standards

TESOL International Association (TESOL) (2020, November 20). TESOL International Association joins more than 1,000 organizations in commitment to advance diversity and inclusion in the workplace [Press release]. https://www.tesol.org/docs/default-source/advocacy/tesol-and-ceo-action-press-release-final796e9942f2fd6d058c49ff00004ecf9b.pdf?sfvrsn=7e93f4dc_0

Thompson, N., & Pascal, J. (2012). Developing critically reflective practice. *Reflective Practice*, 13(2), 311–325. DOI: 10.1080/14623943.2012.657795

Tomaš, Z., Moger, N., Park, A., & Specht, K. (2017). Enriching graduate TESOL methods and materials courses with academic service-learning pedagogy. In T. S. C. Farrell (Ed.), *Preservice teacher education* (pp. 59–65). TESOL Press.

Tulane University Office of Service-Learning (n.d.). http://www.tulane.edu/%7eServLrng/main.shtml

University of Southern Indiana (2020). Service learning outcomes. https://www.usi.edu/outreach/service-learning-program/faculty/service-learning-outcomes/

Uy, S. J. (2019). Infusing service-learning into allied health profession curriculum: perceived enablers and barriers. *Metropolitan Universities Journal*, 30(3), 36–52.

Van Auken, R. (2019, October 10). International service learning: What it is and how it benefits you. Volunteer Forever. https://www.volunteerforever.com/article_post/international-service-learning-what-it-is-and-how-it-benefits-you/

Vanderbilt University Office of Active Citizenship and Learning (n.d.). https://www.vanderbilt.edu/oacs/oacs-global-service-learning-program/ https://www.vanderbilt.edu/search/?q=importance+of+reflection+in+service+learning#gsc.tab=0&gsc.q=importance%20of%20reflection%20in%20service%20learning&gsc.page=1

Van Leeuwen, C. A., Weeks, L. E., Guo-Brennan, L. Y. (2017). Indigenous perspectives on community service-learning in higher education: An examination of the Kenyan context. *International Journal of Research on Service-Learning and Community Engagement*, 5(1), 129–143. http://journals.sfu.ca/iarslce

Waldner, L. S., McGorry, S. Y., & Widener, M. C. (2010). Extreme e-service learning (XE-SL): E-service learning in the 100% online course. *Journal of Online Learning and Teaching*, 6(4), 839–850.

Waldner, L. S., McGorry, S. Y., & Widener, M. C. (2012). E-service-learning: The evolution of service-learning to engage a growing online student population. *Journal of Higher Education Outreach and Engagement*, 16(2), 123–150.

Wang, J., Martin, N., & Stiefvater, E. (n.d.). Beyond the classroom: Service learning in out-of-school time. *Youth Impact*, 3, 1–13.

Ward, J. R., & McCotter, S. S. (2004). Reflection as a visible outcome for preservice teachers. *Teaching and Teacher Education*, 20(3), 243–257.

Wiggins, G., & McTighe, J. (1998). *Understanding by design*. Association for Supervision & Curriculum Development.

Wilhelm, J. D, Baker, T. N., & Dube, J. (2001). *Strategic reading: Guiding students to lifelong literacy 6–12*. Boynton/Cook Publishers.

Wu, C. H. (2015). More than volunteering: Tapping EFL learners' funds of knowledge in a short-term service-learning program in Taiwan. In J. M. Perren, & A. J. Wurr (Eds), *Learning the language of global citizenship: Strengthening service-learning in TESOL* (pp. 503–522). Common Ground Publishing.

Wu, C. H. (2018) Intercultural citizenship through participation in an international service-learning program: A case study from Taiwan. *Language Teaching Research*, 22(5), 517–531.

Wu, C. H., & Dahlgren, R. L. (2011). Discourse of advocacy: Student learners' critical reflections on working with Spanish speaking immigrant students. In T. Stewart & N. Webster (Eds), *Problematizing service-learning: Critical reflections for development and action* (pp. 263–294). Information Age Publishing.

Wurr, A. (2018). Advances in service-learning research with English language learners. *Journal of Service-Learning in Higher Education, 8,* 1–16.

Yang, P. (2015) Developing intercultural competence in TESOL service-learning: Volunteer tutoring for recently-arrived adult refugees in learning English as a Second Language. In J. M. Perren & A. J. Wurr (Eds), *Learning the language of global citizenship: Strengthening service-learning in TESOL* (pp. 331–354). Common Ground Publishing.

Youth Service America (n.d.). *Service, the 4Cs, and employment skills.* https://ysa.org/wp-content/uploads/2016/01/Resource4Cs.pdf

Index